An Open Secret

THE STORY OF DEADWOOD'S
MOST NOTORIOUS BORDELLOS

CHRIS ENSS
AND DEADWOOD HISTORY, INC.

TWODOT®

ESSEX, CONNECTICUT
HELENA, MONTANA

A · TWODOT® · BOOK

An imprint of Globe Pequot, the trade division of
The Rowman & Littlefield Publishing Group, Inc.
4501 Forbes Blvd., Ste. 200
Lanham, MD 20706
www.rowman.com

Distributed by NATIONAL BOOK NETWORK

British Library Cataloguing in Publication Information available

Library of Congress Cataloging-in-Publication Data

Names: Enss, Chris, 1961- author. | Deadwood History, Inc., author.
Title: An open secret : the story of Deadwood's most notorious bordellos / Chris Enss and
  Deadwood History, Inc.
Description: Essex, Connecticut : TwoDot, [2023] | Includes bibliographical references and index.
Identifiers: LCCN 2022042386 (print) | LCCN 2022042387 (ebook) | ISBN 9781493061464
  (paperback ; alk. paper) | ISBN 9781493061471 (ebook)
Subjects: LCSH: Prostitution—South Dakota—Deadwood—History—19th century. | Brothels—
  South Dakota—Deadwood—History—19th century.
Classification: LCC HQ146.D3 E68 2023 (print) | LCC HQ146.D3 (ebook) | DDC
  306.7409783/9109034—dc23/eng/20221021
LC record available at https://lccn.loc.gov/2022042386
LC ebook record available at https://lccn.loc.gov/2022042387

∞™ The paper used in this publication meets the minimum requirements of American National
Standard for Information Sciences—Permanence of Paper for Printed Library Materials, ANSI/
NISO Z39.48-1992.

CONTENTS

Acknowledgments v
Foreword vii
Introduction 1
CHAPTER 1: Al Swearingen and the Gem Variety Theater 19
CHAPTER 2: Madam Eleanora Dumont 41
CHAPTER 3: Madam Mollie Johnson 49
CHAPTER 4: Madam Dora DuFran 61
CHAPTER 5: Madam Alice Ivers 69
CHAPTER 6: Madam Belle Haskell and the Demise of
        Maggie Broadwater 83
CHAPTER 7: Madam May Brown and the Tragic Life and
        Death of Maud Lee 93
CHAPTER 8: The Trials of Thelma Campbell 103
CHAPTER 9: The Murder of Maggie McDermott 109
CHAPTER 10: The End for Women of Easy Virtue in Deadwood . .119
CHAPTER 11: The Last Madam in Deadwood 137
CHAPTER 12: Businesses in the Bad Lands 145
Afterword 157

Notes 159
Bibliography 175
Index 179
About the Author 189

ACKNOWLEDGMENTS

My first debt is to Carolyn Weber and Rose Speirs, at Deadwood History, Inc., for agreeing to pursue the idea of a book on the "soiled doves" of Deadwood Gulch. Their kindness and knowledge made this work possible. It was a joy to collaborate with them.

Others who deserve recognition and thanks are as follows: Halley Hair, researcher at the South Dakota State Archives, without whose unfailing and generous assistance this project could not have been undertaken; Matthew T. Reitzel, manuscript-photo archivist at the South Dakota State Archives; Rachel Lovelace-Portal, curator of collections, Deadwood History, Inc.; Tia Stenson, archivist, Deadwood History, Inc.; Kellen Cutsforth, photo archivist at the Denver Public Library; professional fact checker and freelance wordsmith Barry Williams for making sure all was accurate; graphic artist Jeff Galpin for creating special title pages for the manuscript; author, historian, and friend Linda Wommack for her encouragement and support.

And finally, to the soiled doves who left their mark on the Old West.

FOREWORD

When I was approached by David Milch in 2003 to play the role of "Jewel" in HBO's original series, *Deadwood*, I truthfully did not know much about the real Deadwood, South Dakota, or its history. In my own effort to help create the role I played in the series, Milch gave me a couple of books to read about the Black Hills. Then I actually made a couple of trips to Deadwood, where I continued to learn more about the history and gain a fair amount of knowledge of what life was like in 1876 Deadwood, SD.

Having been to Deadwood, I now have an even deeper understanding of the people of Deadwood then and now. The town and the citizens of Deadwood are survivors. As Chris Enss notes in her book, the town was totally destroyed by fire, and yet it has been rebuilt, again and again, thanks to the perseverance of the human spirit.

Although my fictional character, Jewel, was not a prostitute, I had to breathe life and believability into Milch's vision and my own as to how she would have navigated life and her relationships with the men and women in the Wild West era of Deadwood. Having an obvious disability, Jewel would not have been treated kindly by most people, and if she had had any friendships, they would more than likely have been with whores. These women, like Jewel, were viewed as outcasts and undesirable eyesores of society.

And after reading *An Open Secret*, I am now more aware of what life was really like for the soiled doves of Deadwood. It was fascinating to read about the hardships, the abuse, the fines, the prison time served for the crimes committed, and the battles these women fought just to survive. This book gave names and faces to the women, the madams, and the bordellos of ill repute.

An Open Secret does not glorify the profession of prostitution, but rather presents well-documented and researched portraits of lives that are generally frowned upon in society; individuals judged without really understanding what is actually going on behind the red lights, purple doors, or cozy rooms. The stories also capture the politics, the moral issues of prostitution, and how the nineteenth century shaped the mindset, attitudes, and fabric of America today.

Of course, there are stories of famous characters like Wild Bill. Hickok met his end in Deadwood. Enss covers the infamous murder in the No. 10 Saloon, and how a madam might have changed Wild Bill's fate had she been with him that night.

Also, it was quite interesting to read about the real Al Swearingen, the character that Ian McShane played so brilliantly in the HBO series, *Deadwood*. Yes, he was even more ruthless than I previously understood. He was a shrewd businessman, an abusive pimp, and just as complex as McShane portrayed him in the series.

If you loved the HBO series *Deadwood*, you'll love *An Open Secret* which gives the reader a window into the lives of the "wicked" women of Deadwood, SD. Read on to learn more about their presence in the community, their legal battles, the laws of the land created by men who wished to control these enterprising women.

Geri Jewell
October, 2022

INTRODUCTION

ON JUNE 8, 1876, PHATTY THOMAS, A GRIZZLED, PALE-EYED MULE SKINner, drove his wagon down Deadwood's main thoroughfare toward one of the town's most popular dance halls.[1] In the back of his vehicle was a load of frightened cats that were meowing and hissing. The distressed animals watched the sight pass by them from their crude, wooden crates. The eyes of the scared felines were large and round, their ears were lying back on their heads, and most were huddled into a ball, terrified to be caged and unsure of what was happening.[2]

Phatty proudly smiled at the townspeople who were craning their necks to get a better view of the cargo. When at last he arrived at his destination, several women of ill repute hurried out of the establishment where they worked and happily greeted the cat wrangler. The excited women wasted no time selecting the cat they wanted for their own, and, after paying Phatty between ten and forty dollars for the precious pets, the soiled doves hurried off with their treasures.[3]

Loneliness was the businesswomen's motivation for their purchases. The many men who frequented the brothels and paid them to be their partners for the evening, could not provide the affection and comfort they craved. Theirs was a desperate, sometimes dangerous job, and many women despised being a part of the often-isolated profession. "We are there because we must have bread," a frontier madam once admitted. "The man is there because he must have pleasure; he has no other necessity for being there; true if we were not there the men would not come. But we are not permitted to be anywhere else."[4]

Less than a year after prospector Frank Bryant found gold along the creeks in the narrow mountain-surrounded canyon filled with dead wood in 1875, the town of Deadwood sprung into being. The rush was on. Fortune hunters came staking their claims on the hillsides and gravel beds. Trees were chopped down, and log huts were built. Freight wagons quickly came with their loads of groceries, pianos, wine, whiskey, picks,

A busy Deadwood in 1877 COURTESY OF LIBRARY OF CONGRESS

Main Street of Deadwood in 1877 COURTESY OF DEADWOOD HISTORY, INC. ADAMS
MUSEUM COLLECTION, DEADWOOD, SD

shovels, gold pans, and fine clothes.[5] Most of the clothes were for the
few ladies who followed their husbands west and for the "sporting girls"
who wasted no time opening houses to entertain the hordes flowing into
the region. The unique mixture of people swarming into the Black Hills
created one of the fastest-growing mining communities in the country.
Saloons multiplied beyond necessity; monte and faro games were in full
blast, and strains of inviting music wafted out of the establishments, lur-
ing miners into businesses where they, and their possessions, were soon
parted.

As with all early gold mining camps, Deadwood in the beginning was
a lawless town. Theft and murder were commonplace, and personal safety
routinely depended on the use of firearms. Gambling dens flourished, and
many prostitutes proudly flaunted what they had to sell on street corners

and in alleyways. Rules against such blatant immorality were tolerated but only for a time. Two months after the town officially came into being, well-behaved citizens demanded law and order be instituted.

"The lawlessness in Deadwood Gulch must be ended," announced the editor of the *Deadwood Pioneer Times* in its June 1876 editorial.

> *The situation is becoming intolerable. We are not safe in our tents; our claims are being jumped by roustabouts who come in here believing that they can do anything they want to do. A shooting a night seems to be the rule. The summer air is filled with profanity and curses as men reel and stagger to and from the saloons. The dance hall girls powdered and rouged in their low-necked and sleeveless dresses must be put in their places. They cannot be allowed to loiter along the roads to tempt the hardworking prospectors into their dives, to take from them sacks of gold dust, their grubstake.*[6]
>
> *Arise, citizens, arise! Protect yourselves and your wives and families who soon will be coming into these wild and turbulent gold diggings. We must have law and order and peace.*[7]

The Green Front Theater was one of Deadwood's first brothels. Customers visited soiled doves there via a private entrance in the back of the building. COURTESY OF DEADWOOD HISTORY, INC. ADAMS MUSEUM COLLECTION, DEADWOOD, SD

Curtailing killings and robberies were easier than regulating the vices of whiskey and women. Although prostitution was far from being socially acceptable, it was viewed by many as a necessary evil. The profession was tolerated for two reasons. First, the public believed it prevented randy miners and ranch hands from raping decent women. Second, given that new mothers were expected to refrain from having sex while breastfeeding and that those children were not completely weened until they were two years old, it was commonly accepted that husbands in such situations could seek satisfaction in the arms of the ladies of easy virtue.[8]

Frustrated with the inability to rid Deadwood of prostitutes, editors at the *Daily Champion* newspaper, a competitor of the *Deadwood Pioneer Times*, suggested in an article in the June 9, 1877, edition of the publication that brothels be removed from the most popular streets and avenues and relegated only to alleyways and out-of-the-way locations.

If we have to tolerate houses of ill repute, it becomes a duty incumbent on every good citizen, and especially the officers of the law, to see to it that such houses are removed from our leading thoroughfares and that the principals be restrained from advertising their calling on thoroughfares where the wives, daughters, and families of our people are compelled to daily traverse.[9]

Legend has it that some of the first fallen ladies in Deadwood arrived in the same caravan with lawman James Butler Hickok, wagon master Charlie Utter, and frontierswoman Calamity Jane in July 1876. A few of those ladies opened their own brothels, and others went to work for businesses already established in town. Many were employed at hurdy-gurdy houses. A hurdy-gurdy is a musical instrument with strings that vibrate by a resin wheel turned by a crank and shortened at will by keys operated by the fingers of the player.[10] The women that worked at the hurdy-gurdy houses performed high kicking, prancing dances that appealed to lonesome miners. Hurdy-gurdy girls charged the men for each dance and persuaded the men to buy them drinks. The hurdy-gurdy houses and many of the brothels were located in a section of town called the Bad Lands.[11]

The area in Deadwood where most of the brothels were located was known as the Bad Lands. Photograph was taken in 1877 COURTESY OF DEADWOOD HISTORY, INC. ADAMS MUSEUM COLLECTION, DEADWOOD, SD

Among the most notable Deadwood soiled doves, or supposed soiled doves, in 1876 and 1877 were Belle McMahon, Jenny Hines, and DiGee, also known as China Doll. Belle was frequently arrested and charged with prostitution. Jenny Hines, also known as Popcorn Jenny, was apprehended several times for operating a bawdy house. An incident that occurred on February 21, 1877, marked the beginning of the end of Jenny in Deadwood. Police raided her business after a complaint was made by neighbors about the numerous men coming and going from the location at all hours of the day and night.[12]

When the police arrived on the scene, Jenny reluctantly allowed them to enter. Initially, they found no one in the home apart from the sporting gal herself. She assured the officers that nothing unseemly ever transpired in her home and that the idea she was exchanging sex for money was offensive. A further inspection of the premises resulted in a unique discovery made in her kitchen. The room was void of the traditional items one would expect to find. There were no table and chairs, etc. Instead, on the floor was a mattress and, on the mattress, a man by the name of Joe Hodges. He was under a blanket and curled up in a fetal position, hoping no one could see him. He didn't stir until the police poked him with a cane. Both Joe and Jenny were arrested and taken to jail.[13]

Joe Hodges was brought before the judge not long after the magistrate had dealt with Popcorn Jenny and encouraged her to leave town. Joe was forced to undergo a series of embarrassing questions about why he was doing business with a known prostitute. The only explanation he offered was that he was a "widower and, in obedience to the Scriptural injunction, he was seeking a congenial companion." He claimed when he saw Jenny, he was so charmed by her that he allowed her to lead him astray. He didn't understand why the city would bother with two lonely people helping one another.[14]

The judge admonished Joe and fined him ten dollars. Jenny was never heard from again in Deadwood.[15]

DiGee never ran afoul of the law. She was not, as some people suggested at the time, a prostitute. She was a wealthy woman, and Deadwood residents speculated her money wasn't acquired honestly. Most of the complaints against DiGee were more about her ethnicity, and some believed she provided the funds to advertise in newspapers in the Chinese section of town. According to the June 9, 1877, edition of the *Daily Champion*, respectable citizens objected to the promotion of such services.[16]

There are a number of China women in the lower part of the city blazonly advertising their nefarious calling. . . . Indeed, there are a number of houses on Lee Street filled with the demi-monde,[17] who daily and nightly ply their shameful vocation in the face of the public. The conduct of these women is one of the most notorious features in

7

Deadwood social life. These degraded women stand in their doors and beckon into their lecherous house, all classes of men, some of them the chief businessmen of Deadwood. And the crying shame of it is that the virtuous and pure women of Deadwood are compelled to face this criminal degradation in passing from Main Street to and from the post office on Sherman Street.[18]

Although those who ran houses of ill repute were fined for the illegal activities and the collected fines then passed along to schools and other such public programs, polite society believed their existence had a demoralizing effect on the "moral sentiment of the community" and demanded they be closed. The moral community objected to the streets being "filled with the demi-monde," but they were opposed to the male prostitutes[19] "lurking in alleyways," and disapproved of female gamblers cheating and stealing money from unsuspecting patrons at saloons.[20]

Civic-minded Deadwood residents established courts as soon as they could and set about to gain control of the wrongdoings, but the first, unofficial law enforcement agents proved to be less than honest. The police were in league with the gamblers who ruled the town and the criminals who evaded justice. Until strong men of good moral character were hired to bring order to the gold town, chaos ruled.[21] A feature story in the September 11, 1877, edition of *Frank Leslie's Weekly* highlighted the lack of law and order in the rough burg.[22]

Deadwood City, in the Dakota division of the Black Hills region, is one of the liveliest and queerest places west of the Mississippi. It has grown more rapidly than any of the other new mining camps and, in the space of two years, has attained a fixed population of 4,000, and a floating citizenship of 2,000 more.[23]

All in all, there's not much law and order in Deadwood. The saloon men refuse to pay their licenses, $100, and defy the law. Claim jumpers and town-lot jumpers have things pretty much their own way. Innocent boys and gentlemanly road agents abound. The man who would cut your throat for a few dollars, or the gentlemanly fellow who would rope you into bunko or other games and call it the square

thing to take all they can from you lies in wait. And then there's the
soiled doves and their businesses. The publicity of so many houses of
prostitution is out of control.[24]

It was only when hotel and hardware store owner Seth Bullock was appointed sheriff of Lawrence County by the governor of the Dakota Territory in the spring of 1877 that some semblance of order started to take hold. Murders, claim jumping, highway robbery, drunk and disorderly behavior and the like weren't readily tolerated. Criminals were charged, and cases were routinely argued in a makeshift courtroom in the upper story of the post office building. Most illegal activities were prosecuted to the full extent, but prostitutes and brothel owners guilty of violations were treated less severely. Prominent citizens who frequented such establishments and whose visits and drunken conduct were reported in one of three Deadwood newspapers were often forgiven of their dalliances by paying a fine and offering a public apology. With law enforcement and the judicial system choosing to give prostitution a pass, churches stepped in to address the issue. In April 1881, a committee of the City Council of Deadwood (many of those members were ministers or missionaries) recommended that an ordinance be passed regarding bawdy houses and gambling dens that would prevent them from doing any business on the Sabbath. The committee was convinced such an ordinance would improve the morals of the town.[25]

On May 20, 1881, the staff at the *Black Hills Daily Times* ran an editorial on the matter and argued that the social evil was one no legislation could correct as long as there were unhappy men. It was the paper's position that only working women would suffer as a result of the proposed ordinance and called upon the law to deal harshly with men who patronized such businesses every day of the week.[26]

While we advocate the regulation of these establishments, while we
would have those who violate common decency, the women we mean
punished, while they should be compelled to keep good order, which they
are apt to do of their own accord for their own interests, we would go
still further and make the law more comprehensive. In certain cities, a

favorite method of replenishing a depleted treasury is to raid houses of ill-fame, arrest the inmates, and fine the inmates.[27]

No laws can reach the moral nature of anyone, a badman is no better or worse in his inherent nature with or without law. These enactments may, in part, restrain him from giving free play to his vicious nature, but do not reform him. The laws against unfortunate women are partial, and we think radically unjust. Of course, if a woman is so debased and degraded as to solicit the sale of her favors on the public streets, she should be immediately abated as a public, disgraceful nuisance. But only the fewest number do this, the majority remain in their own homes and conduct themselves, so far as decorum is concerned, in as quiet and ladylike manner as the best in the city.[28]

So far as commercial honesty and liberality are concerned, no inhabitants of this city are most prompt and reliable. It is but right these unfortunate women who have fallen under the social ban should have all the credit due them, for few enough have a word said in their favor. For their morals, their vicious examples, and their horrible profession, we have only words of severe condemnation. We should be just, and speaking in that light, when we examine the ordinance regulating these scarlet women, we fail to discover entire justice; we discover that they alone are amenable to law, while their patrons, men who sustain and support them, who frequent their houses and nine times out of ten create the disturbances that are raised there, are allowed to go scot-free, without fine or penalty. We maintain this is gross injustice, a grievous wrong.[29]

There were many people living in the Black Hills region who believed nothing could ultimately be done to eliminate bawdy houses or those that worked there. They declared such efforts hopeless, a waste of the court's time, and a fruitless expense. Soiled doves, such as the noted Lou Polk who had a bawdy house in Wyoming, decided to relocate to Deadwood after learning how much more amenable they were to women in their line of work than in Casper. The continued influx of prostitutes to the Black Hills area prompted concerned family men to voice their opinions on the disgraceful manner in which the public affairs in the county were being handled. Accusations were made that authorities had turned their heads to prostitution because various political parties were benefitting monetarily by allowing saloons and houses of ill repute to continue operating.[30]

"Last spring a low dance house dive was opened on the business center of Main Street and a dozen prostitutes employed to parade the streets and assist certain officers in drumming up business for the establishment," a letter to the editor of the *Black Hills Union* on the topic read. "The respectable ladies of the city, in order to protect their school children from example and insults of the pimps and harlots who carried on their business at that dive, petitioned the public officers, city and county, to enforce the prohibition law against that dance house and inmates, or if this would be too much to ask, then to compel them to carry on the business in a less public manner and in a less public place, but the city and county officers, after a short consideration, refused the petition and in substance informed them that they had no right in the matter at least that pimps and prostitutes were bound to respect."[31]

Authorities who tried to uphold the laws against prostitution often found themselves in physical altercations with the accused women. Such was the case with soiled doves Florence Winters and Lora Waldon. The pair horsewhipped an attorney who pressed charges on the women in September 1892. When the abused lawyer finally managed to get away from the pair, they pelted him with eggs.[32]

On Friday, December 9, 1892, five women were brought before circuit court judge John P. Belding for refusing to pay the five-dollar fines they owed for violating the ordinance regulating prostitution. Two of the professional women claimed to be actresses who worked at the Gem Variety Theater. They insisted they weren't prostitutes but worked for a salary performing. The "actresses" informed the judge they had no intention of paying anything because they were innocent. Judge Belding didn't believe their claim and had them incarcerated until such time they saw fit to pay up. They called for their employer at the Gem Variety Theater, and he hurried to the performers' aid. As their cases were not bailable, his only recourse was to pay their fines, which he did under protest, promising to test the validity of the law on the matter of fining prostitutes.[33]

A week later Judge Belding was back in court reviewing the complaints and warrants against four "notorious" sporting women who had traveled from Rapid City to Deadwood to work. The women brought before his bench had been charged with violating laws against prostitution. They had been arrested by a marshal who refused to overlook the crime. The women were combative and pointed out to the court that most officers let them go with a simple warning. The judge could not be persuaded to do the same and was adamant that women in their vocation needed to have respect for the law and the dignity of the city.[34]

The fines collected from prostitution in a given month in Deadwood could be substantial. According to the Deadwood City Council minutes from January 6, 1893, more than $3,500 in fines had been paid by soiled doves or their madams and pimps in 1892.[35]

A number of the sporting women in Deadwood frequently found themselves in trouble with the law for reasons that had nothing to do with running an illegal house or failure to pay a fine. Prostitutes accused one another of stealing their possessions or money; they fought over customers, stole from their customers, or were tossed out of legitimate businesses for using obscene language.[36]

In August 1894, deputies arrived on the scene of a violent dispute between a prostitute named Maggie Davis and two patrons of the business where Maggie worked. The incident took place at a brothel located above the Fish and Hunter grocery store. Maggie and a few of her coworkers were drinking with a few men who had stopped by to enjoy their company. A fight broke out between Maggie and one of the other women. Maggie's customer tried to break up the fight, and she grabbed a hatchet and struck him twice in the head. He punched her, knocking her down a flight of stairs. Maggie was stunned but picked herself up and ran out of the house. The customer followed her, carrying a bottle with him. He threw the bottle at her as he was running, and it struck her just above the left temple. Two other men doing business at the house hurried after the man who had hit Maggie. They tackled the man, and he kicked and squirmed to try and get away. They hit him in the head with a rock and knocked him unconscious. Both Maggie and the assailant were arrested and taken to jail.[37]

Working women like Maggie, taken into custody for "raising a disturbance," had to spend more than a day in jail and pay a fine of $12.50. Other soiled doves, such as Otie James, who refused to pay fines on similar charges, hired a lawyer to represent them in court. The penalty for not accepting guilt and troubling the court with the matter was severe. Otie's fine was increased to one hundred dollars, and she was detained in jail until she could pay the full amount.[38]

Not only was the possibility of assault ever present for prostitutes, but unwanted pregnancies, general diseases, and even death often resulted by entertaining numerous men. Some prostitutes escaped the hell of the trade by committing suicide. Some drank themselves to death; others overdosed on laudanum. Lizzie Paine, a well-known soiled dove in Deadwood with frizzy, bleached hair, tried to kill herself in October 1895 by using a heavy dose of morphine.[39] A doctor was quickly called to the scene to help rid her system of the poison, and she made a full recovery. Mrs. I. Sessions, another noted Black Hills character who worked as a prostitute and dealt cards, attempted suicide using poison in July 1886. According to the *Black Hills Weekly Herald*, "She had been absent for several weeks and returned, appearing to be in a very despondent frame of mind." No reason was given as to why she sought to end her life.[40]

By the latter part of the 1800s, the respectable women of Deadwood had decided to band together to confront the issue of prostitution and the destruction associated with the profession. Known as the Deadwood Woman's Vigilance Committee, the group resolved to "rid the town of prostitutes that try in any way to make trouble in families by separating the husband and wife and disgracing their innocent children." The committee gave the soiled doves one month to leave Deadwood. If the women refused to leave voluntarily, the committee vowed to have them forcibly removed.[41]

"Our city officers are very careful to drive all the tramps and vagrant persons from our town," a spokeswoman for the committee told the local press, "but they leave worse villains than tramps unmolested. They leave villainous women who are a disgrace to their sex." When all was said and done, the soiled doves and their businesses remained.[42]

13

View of Deadwood's main thoroughfare from the Bad Lands, 1896. COURTESY OF
DEADWOOD HISTORY, INC. ADAMS MUSEUM COLLECTION, DEADWOOD, SD

As the nineteenth century gave way to the twentieth, houses of ill
repute and the prostitutes who worked in them remained under attack
from Deadwood citizens, politicians, and business owners who insisted
the brothels be shut down. This was in spite of the fact that many madams
had purchased licenses to operate their houses. The practice of requiring
ladies of the evening to obtain a license had begun in Deadwood in early
1890. The majority of the soiled doves complied with the mandate, but
others adamantly refused.[43]

According to the September 26, 1896, edition of the *Black Hills Weekly
Times*, "More than one-half of the cost of maintaining local courts and
police forces were caused directly or indirectly by the element of sporting
women in town." Taxpayers were annoyed with the heavy expense created by the prostitutes and believed the women should contribute more
toward maintaining the government of the city.[44]

City officials argued that in order for the licensing system to work and not be a drain on Deadwood residents, all sporting women had to pay once a year for a license. Any house operating without a license was subject to being closed. That directive was a difficult one to impose. The prostitutes who wouldn't purchase a license had rooms in the upper stories of business blocks, and various other secret locations, and law enforcement couldn't readily find them. To make up for those prostitutes evading the rules, prostitutes who did obey the law were charged extra for a license when they reapplied. Those prostitutes accused the city of discriminating against them and searched for a way to work around the order.[45]

The longer the problem of prostitution persisted the more residents complained and sought to take matters into their own hands. Madams hired security guards to protect their girls and their businesses from forced closures by private citizens. The monthly payment for a security force was thirty to fifty dollars.[46]

Frustrated townspeople who took exception to the courts simply issuing fines and continuing to allow bawdy house owners, who repeatedly violated the law, to remain open voiced their opinions in local newspapers.

"The practice of virtually licensing prostitution by the collection of so-called 'fines' at stated intervals and putting money into the public treasury is unacceptable," wrote a citizen to the editor of the *Daily Deadwood Pioneer Times* in May 1902. "I do not believe the good people of Deadwood desire to share in the earnings of prostitutes or to have the expenses of the city paid with funds so obtained. The social evil is a most difficult problem to deal with. It seems almost impossible to suppress it, and the best we can hope for is to keep it in the shadows and not permit it to be flaunted. But to make it a source of revenue is a shame and a disgrace to any city or people."[47]

Members of the Woman's Christian Temperance Union (WCTU) let the community know their position on the issue of sex workers in Deadwood and the inefficiency of the city police in a letter to the editors at the *Daily Deadwood Pioneer Times* in January 1900. They resented the streets of the town being taken over by "drunken, foul-mouthed male and female prostitutes." WCTU members warned that unless some efforts were made to improve conditions, the police could expect organized protests against the morality and obvious corruption within the police force.[48]

Such threats had an impact, albeit short lived. Law enforcement did make sure the streets of Deadwood were clear of soiled doves and inebriated men after ten o'clock, but houses of ill repute did not cease to exist. Deadwood's prostitution problem still loomed large, and several professional women continued their practices of refusing to pay their monthly licenses.

In March 1902, police raided several houses of prostitution in the Bad Lands, taking into custody a number of bawdy women who owed the city of Deadwood money. A suffragette submitted a letter to the editor of the *Weekly Pioneer Times* expressing why she felt the arrests were discriminatory.[49]

"I have wondered why these gentlemen [local politicians] allow wine rooms and dance halls to exist," Mrs. Florence R. Curruthers wrote on March 6, 1902. "Are they for men only? Do you think women would go there if they didn't expect the men to be there, and don't the men expect the women to be there, or take them there? Why are not the men who frequent these places on the same level as the women not fined just the same? Perhaps it would place some of the respected citizens and perhaps an officer of the law in an embarrassing position at times. Because some of these gentlemen have been allowed to enter these places (by mistake, of course) and take a few drops with a gentleman friend. Now if they are allowed to run for traps, fine the men, too, and we could soon have asphalt walks and streets, instead of dilapidated excuses we have at present.[50]

"Prostitution exists among the men as well as the women. Women prostitutes exist because there are men prostitutes. This is not an argument in defense of prostitution among women, but I believe in fair play. If you are going to enforce the law, enforce it, and not only half do it, by excluding the men."[51]

Owing to the combined efforts of temperance workers, members of the clergy, and concerned parents' groups, the issue of prostitution became less of a problem between 1903 and 1905. The criminal element that had been omnipresent since Deadwood came into existence, for a time, kept themselves off the main thoroughfares of town and out of sight from polite society.

"Never in the history of Deadwood has the outlook for our city been so bright as the present," an editorial in the September 28, 1905, edition of the *Daily Deadwood Pioneer Times* began about the civility that had overtaken the area.

> *The present tone of public sentient assures us a clean, moral atmo-sphere, wherein people need not fear to invest their money and build homes. Business interests have already taken a cue from this improved sentiment and are investing their money in building up the town. Just let the average man contemplate for a moment the large number of valuable enterprises now under way, or assured in the near future, and then let him ask himself if the change in moral sentiment has been a detriment or a benefit to the city?[52]*
>
> *Business instinct in this matter is unerring. Men do not invest their money, nor people build homes in a town run by pimps, gamblers,*

Soiled doves pose for a picture in 1905. AUTHOR'S COLLECTION

and prostitutes. And just in proportion as we weed out these disreputable elements will our city flourish and become what its location and resources designed that it should be. Labor is all employed, and the crows of loafers which formerly blocked the sidewalks and saloons are conspicuous by their absence.[53]

In time, the sins that contributed to Deadwood's reputation as a wild and uncivilized town reemerged from the shadows and the war against the brothels that flourished there raged on another seventy-five years.

1

AL SWEARINGEN AND THE GEM VARIETY THEATER

THE GEM VARIETY THEATER WAS OVERFLOWING WITH CURIOUS CLIEN-
tele, all there to see eight-year-old performer Mary A. McDonald, better
known as Baby McDonald. It was the summer of 1877, and the popular,
diminutive star was sharing the stage with her father, James, the origina-
tor of skate and pedestal dancing. Miners, business owners, their families,
ladies, and children filled every available seat. The audience erupted in
applause when the talent alighted from the wings to begin their act.[1]

Al Swearingen, the owner of the theater, a short, husky, fiendish-
looking man with greasy black hair and a black slicked-down mustache,
watched the excitement unfold from behind a nearby bar. His taurine
eyes glittered at the sight of the number of people in his establishment. A
sold-out crowd meant a substantial profit for the evening. Baby McDonald was a great draw, and the amusement-loving people of the Black Hills
responded liberally to the petite attraction.[2]

Given the variety of ticket buyers enjoying the show, a passerby might
believe there was nothing objectional about the Gem. Like Swearingen,
in which the only agreeable thing about him was the tailor-made, three-
piece suits he wore, the least offensive activity at the theater was the innocent song and dance routine presented by the little girl on stage.

The second floor of the building was reserved for Swearingen's stable
of prostitutes. Men from every occupation visited the women who worked
there. Some of those women were willing participants, and others were
lured into the trade, having traveled to the Black Hills on the pretense
of being an actress at the Gem Variety Theater. Swearingen frequently

Unknown prostitute strikes a daring pose to entice potential customer
AUTHOR'S COLLECTION

Gem Variety Theater and Dance Hall in 1895. The Gem was owned and operated by Al Swearingen. COURTESY OF DEADWOOD HISTORY, INC. ADAMS MUSEUM COLLECTION, DEADWOOD, SD

visited major East Coast locations looking for female entertainers. Aspiring actresses, singers, and dancers enthusiastically responded to the call; when they arrived in Deadwood, they learned there were no jobs performing on stage. Void of prospects and lacking the funds to return home, the desperate women succumbed to working for Swearingen in his brothel.[3]

Born in Mahaska, Iowa, on July 8, 1845, entrepreneur Ellis Alfred Swearingen arrived in Deadwood in May 1876 with his wife, Nettie, and an unnamed young man. The trio had relocated from Custer City in the Dakota Territory when news that gold had been discovered. Swearingen had operated a house of ill repute in Custer City with fourteen prostitutes in his employ. Two of those professionals were his wife and the man who accompanied him to Deadwood Gulch. Before investing in the Gem, Swearingen opened the Cricket Saloon. The Cricket was a small-scale

Interior of the Gem Variety Theater. COURTESY OF DEADWOOD HISTORY, INC. ADAMS MUSEUM COLLECTION, DEADWOOD, SD

tavern where nightly boxing matches were held. By April 1877, he had sold the saloon and opened the Gem Variety Theater.[4]

Before hiring a stable of women to work in his upstairs bordello, Swearingen's wife and the man who traveled with them to town kept company with the paying customers. Nettie floated about the saloon introducing herself to the patrons. Her coworker, dressed in women's clothing and wearing a wig, served drinks. Both helped provide the funds to pay respectable acts to perform on the spacious stage sandwiched between the bar and a row of curtained boxes. Those boxes, which were essentially small rooms, were used by struggling dancers to spend time with the most prosperous Black Hills patrons.[5]

From the start, the Gem was one of the most popular enterprises in the region. "Al Swearingen is doing a driving business at his new Variety Theater," an article in the April 21, 1877, edition of the *Black Hills Weekly Pioneer* informed the public. "Delighted audiences assemble there nightly with the minstrel music, ballad singing, banjo playing, bone rattling, tambo whacking, comic acts, numerous scenes, sketches, refrains, droll doings, and diversions that make up a first-class variety performance." In addition to the well-known talent regularly performing at the establishment, Swearingen hosted grand masquerade balls at the theater. Residents flocked to the business that, on the surface, appeared above reproach.[6]

Swearingen was gracious and inviting to the legitimate entertainers who played his theater and who attracted large audiences, but he wasn't as generous to the moneymakers who were soiled doves. He wasn't opposed to verbally abusing or assaulting them. He encouraged customers to do the same if the women got out of line. When Swearingen wasn't available to take a heavy-handed approach with the prostitutes, he left the job to two men he hired to manage his affairs. Both Dan Dority, the general manager of the Gem, and Johnny Burns, placed in charge of the sporting girls, beat the women whenever they felt it was necessary. Other employees of Swearingen's, such as Edward Trimpy, were given permission to punch and kick the prostitutes as well. Trimpy became so accustomed to the women at the Gem cowering and not fighting back he assumed women of ill repute everywhere would respond the same. In late December 1877, a soiled dove named Kitty "Tricks" Sparrow stood up to Swearingen's hired hand. It happened at nine in the morning at the Pearl Saloon on Main Street. Trimpy was getting ready to return to the Gem after spending the evening with Kitty when she accused him of stealing a ten dollar bill from her. He denied the charge and threatened to "bang" her if she repeated it. Kitty informed him that he "wasn't going to bang anyone." She then stepped behind the bar and removed a pistol hidden under the counter and leveled it at him. Outraged, Trimpy raced around the counter to take the weapon from her. She shot him before he got to her. The bullet struck the man in the right cheek near the nose. It passed through the back of his head where it then lodged.[7]

Trimpy fell to the ground and was quickly carried to his room in the rear of the Gem. A doctor was called to the scene but was unable to remove the bullet from the injured man's head. Trimpy died shortly after the examination. Kitty was taken into custody and charged with murder. She was upset Trimpy had died but did not regret her actions.[8]

Trimpy's brutal demise did not prompt Swearingen to curtail the harsh treatment of the women in his hire. The prostitutes who dared defy his orders often sported black eyes or bruises on their necks and arms. The women were made to fulfill their jobs if they were physically able to do so. Among the duties the soiled doves were to perform once they enticed men into the saloon was to persuade the men to have a drink and spin them around the dance floor. Customers were charged ten cents for a dance, twenty cents for a beer, and one dollar for a bottle of wine.[9]

The appalling way Al Swearingen treated the harlots who worked for him did not go unnoticed by the caring men and women of Deadwood. John S. McClintock, an early pioneer of the Black Hills who knew Swearingen and the Gem, likened the soiled doves to white slaves. He described them as a "motley crew of ungainly features and uncertain ages" and added that "those who failed to measure up to his [Swearingen] requirements as classy attractions were peremptorily discarded and put out, if not forcibly kicked out, on the streets to take refuge in brothels or other places where the management was not wholly devoid of all sense of human feeling."[10]

Some of the women in Swearingen's stable chose to take their own lives rather than continue in the situation they found themselves. John McClintock wrote about one of those women in his book *Pioneer Days in the Black Hills*. She was a teenager living in the East who answered an ad for a singer at the Gem. Upon meeting the young woman on one of his East Coast trips, Swearingen quickly surmised she lacked the financial means to pursue her career. He purchased a ticket on a stage to transport her to Deadwood where she believed she would eventually be the main act at the Gem Variety Theater. One of the first nights working at the business as a dancer, Swearingen demanded she entertain a few men in one of the curtained boxes next to the stage. The naïve woman was strong-armed into drinking champagne and ended up getting drunk and passing out. She awoke the next morning mortified over the fact that the men had taken advantage of her. She shot herself the following day.[11]

During Swearingen's career as a brothel owner in Deadwood, he seldom had occasion to answer for his crimes against women, but he was arrested for brawling with men. On August 18, 1877, he was taken into custody for "assault and battery." Swearingen and a saloon patron tussled over the price of a shot of whiskey. Swearingen insisted the customer owed $1.50 for the drink he'd been served, but the man refused to pay. Blows were exchanged and law enforcement had to step in to settle the matter.[12]

Swearingen again ran afoul of the law for his harsh treatment of a patron in the summer of 1878. Thomas Clark, a miner employed at the Old Abe Mine, spent the evening of Monday, June 24, at the Gem Variety Theater drinking and visiting with women on the second floor. It was late when he returned to the bar and decided to have a few drinks. The more he drank the more abusive he became with the other customers. Swearingen confronted Clark and two began throwing punches, with Swearingen getting the best of the drunk. Clark was battered and bruised when he was tossed out of the theater. Furious, he hurried to get a gun; once he'd acquired a pistol, he marched back into the Gem. The inebriated man warned Swearingen he was armed and told the brothel owner to strap a gun on and meet him outside. Before Clark reached the door, Swearingen stopped him and severely beat him around the face and head with his fists. Swearingen was later arrested for assault, but then released on a $250 bond.[13]

Swearingen's abusive practices came close to his losing the Gem Variety Theater in October 1877 when he was sued by a miner he'd physically beaten while the two were playing cards. The business owner was ordered to pay the victim more than $500, but Swearingen refused. To satisfy the debt, the sheriff ordered the theater sold at an auction in January 1878. Swearingen ultimately paid the amount owed, maintaining ownership of the notorious establishment and the prostitutes who worked for him.[14]

Historians note that early in Swearingen's career as the proprietor of a brothel, two infamous ladies did business for him. Calamity Jane (Martha Jane Canary) and Kitty Alton (Arnold), both known for dressing like men and carrying guns, were among the stable of women employed at the Gem. Unlike the many broken souls intimidated into staying with Swearingen, Kitty and Calamity broke away. Kitty opened her own bordello in Lead, South Dakota, three miles southwest of Deadwood. Her business did well, and she invested some of the profits in various mining companies. Those investments paid off handsomely, and she purchased a ranch outside Custer City. She later married and had children. Calamity left Swearingen's employ to pursue her own interests, namely gambling, traveling occasionally with the army, and driving a stage.[15]

Swearingen's wife, Nettie, eventually left the Gem too. Weary of her husband's violent outbursts, which generally resulted in her getting beaten, she decided to take the matter to the authorities. On December 17, 1879, Nettie swore out a warrant for abuse against her husband. According to an article in the *Daily Deadwood Pioneer Times*, both her eyes were black and her face "pounded almost into jelly" when she brought her petition to the court. Swearingen was arrested, fined $50, and put under a $500 bond to keep peace for a year. The pair divorced shortly after Nettie's complaint was made public.[16]

Customers at the bar in the Gem Variety Theater. The third man from the right standing behind the bar is thought to be Al Swearingen. COURTESY OF DEADWOOD HISTORY, INC. ADAMS MUSEUM COLLECTION, DEADWOOD, SD

During the first three years of the Gem Variety Theater's existence, there was no shortage of newspaper articles describing the violence that took place at the establishment. Whether it was a prostitute taking her own life, miners shooting one another, or the owner of the business assaulting women or drunks, the Gem had a reputation for being a "defiler of youth and a destroyer of home ties." There were instances of violence even among the entertainers hired to perform. Irish dancer Kitty LeRoy accepted Al Swearingen's invitation to appear at the theater in May 1877. She attracted a fair share of attention with her gypsylike costumes, spectacular diamond earrings, and vivacious personality on stage. She was so well-received by the residents of Deadwood that other establishments hired her to work for them when she wasn't dancing at the Gem. During Kitty's seven-month stay in Deadwood, enamored miners competed for her attention, but none held her interest. It wasn't until she met the card sharp Sam Curley that the thought of spending an extended period of time with one special person seemed appealing.[17]

Thirty-five-years-old, Sam Curley was a card sharp with a reputation as a peaceful man who felt more at home behind a poker table than anywhere else. Kitty and Sam had a lot in common, and their mutual attraction blossomed into a proposal of marriage. On June 10, 1877, the pair exchanged vows at the Gem on the same stage where Kitty performed. Unbeknownst to the cheering onlookers and the groom, however, Kitty was already married. Her first husband lived in Bay City, Michigan, with their son who had been born in 1872. Bored with the trappings of a traditional home life, Kitty had abandoned the pair to travel the West.[18] When Sam learned that he was married to a bigamist, he was upset. The newlyweds quarreled, and Sam left Deadwood and headed to Colorado.

Perhaps it was because she was distraught over the abrupt departure of her current husband, but Kitty's congenial personality suddenly turned cold and unfriendly. Distrusting of patrons, she began carrying six-shooters in her skirt pockets and a knife in the folds of the deep curls of her hair. She moved from Deadwood to Central City, where she ran a saloon. Because she was always heavily armed, she was able to keep the wild residents who frequented her establishment under control.[19]

Restless and unable to get beyond Sam's absence, Kitty returned to Deadwood and opened a combination brothel and gambling parlor. She called her place The Mine and enticed many miners to her faro table where she quickly relieved them of their gold dust. On one particularly profitable evening she raked in more than $8,000.[20]

Kitty's profession and seductive manner of dress sparked rumors that she had many lovers and had been married five times. Kitty never denied the rumors and even added to them by boasting that she had been courted by hundreds of eligible bachelors and "lost track of the numbers of times men had proposed" to her. Because she always carried a variety of weapons on her, rumors also abounded that she had shot or stabbed more than a dozen gamblers for cheating at cards. She never denied those tales, either.[21]

By the fall of 1877, the torch Kitty carried for Sam was temporarily extinguished by a former lover. The two spent many nights at another establishment in town known as the Lone Star Saloon and eventually moved in together.[22] News of Kitty's romantic involvement reached a miserable Sam who had established a faro game at a posh saloon in Cheyenne, Wyoming. Sam was furious about being replaced and immediately purchased a ticket back to Deadwood. Hoping to catch Kitty alone with her lover, he disguised his looks and changed his name.[23]

When Sam arrived in town on December 6, 1877, he couldn't bring himself to face the pair in person. He sent a message to Kitty's paramour to meet with him instead, but the man refused. In a fit of rage, Sam told one of the Lone Star Saloon's employees that he intended to kill his unfaithful wife and then himself.[24]

Frustrated and desperate, Sam sent a note to Kitty pleading with her to meet him at the Lone Star Saloon. She reluctantly agreed. Not long after Kitty ascended the stairs of the tavern, patrons heard her scream, followed by the sounds of two gunshots.[25]

A reporter for the *Black Hills Weekly Times* visited the scene of the murder-suicide the morning after the event occurred. "The bodies were dressed and lying side by side in the room of death," he later wrote in an article for the newspaper. "Suspended upon the wall, a pretty picture of Kitty, taken when the bloom and vigor of youth gazed down upon the tenements of clay, as if to enable the visitor to contrast a happy past with a most wretched present. The pool of blood rested upon the floor; blood stains were upon the door and walls. . . . The cause of the tragedy may be summed up in a few words; aye, in one, 'jealousy.'"[26]

The headline of the September 26, 1879, edition of the *Press and Daily Dakotaian* announced that Deadwood was in ashes. A fire that started by an oil lantern at the Star Bakery in town at 2:20 in the morning burned everything of value. The Gem Variety Theater was one of more than three hundred buildings destroyed. Three months prior to the fires, Swearingen had invested in renovating the business and held a grand reopening featuring a myriad of entertainers from Illinois.[27]

"The Gem, which has been thoroughly renovated, and fitted up next to a new pin, was crowded to its fullest capacity until an early hour this morning by a delighted audience," the June 27, 1879, edition of the *Black Hills Daily Times* read.

> *The performance was vastly superior to any variety entertainment ever before given in Deadwood. The selection of songs was all new and good, the jokes were new, the dancing was way-up, new stage scenery, in fact everything is different there now from what we have been accustomed to look upon at our variety theatres heretofore, and if Manager Swearingen does not succeed with his present company, then good-bye to the variety business in the metropolis.*[28]

On October 5, 1879, Swearingen welcomed construction workers to the property to begin rebuilding after the fire. The new theater would be thirty by one hundred feet in dimension with exterior walls twenty-four feet high. Swearingen wanted the structure completed as quickly as money and men could manage. His goal was to have the finest theater building ever erected in Deadwood. By Christmas 1879, patrons were flooding back into the spacious and pristine Gem.[29] The grand reopening of the business took place on New Year's Eve. According to a reporter at the *Weekly Pioneer Times*, the "private boxes and galleries overflowed with the crowd." The reporter also noted that female guests in attendance were dressed in magnificent costumes and wore fine jewelry. The men who escorted the elegantly adorned ladies wore fine suits with high colored shirts and black ties.[30]

"The performance offered to the audience would have been a very fair variety entertainment in Chicago or St. Louis," the January 1, 1880, edition of the *Black Hills Daily Times* read.

One feature, the shooting of Don and Ella Howe. He is a burly, black-haired, grim-faced fellow; she a slender, graceful little creature, seemingly wholly unsuited for the part she plays. With a 42-calibre rifle at a distance of ten paces, he shoots glass balls from her head; then tears a potato from her hand; knocks another from her shoulder; fires at an apple held in her mouth and sends the fragments flying in every direction; and, at last, winds up, while all the audience shouts, 'Stop! Don't try it!' by shooting a large glass earring from her ear.[31]

Al Swearingen sits next to his wife in front of the Gem Variety Theater in the buggy to the left. Johnny Burns, Swearingen's "herder" of prostitutes is in the buggy to the right. Photo was taken between 1880 and 1897. COURTESY OF DEADWOOD HISTORY, INC. ADAMS MUSEUM COLLECTION, DEADWOOD, SD

The Gem's decor was sophisticated, the wallpaper tasteful, the lengthy bar polished to a high gloss, the blue glass oil lamps that lined the stage were modern and effective. All the refinements and famous talent Swearingen brought into the theater attracted business. On a good night he made between $5,000 and $10,00. Comic stars such as Thomas Jefferson and Oscar Willis kept audiences laughing, and cancan dancers, trained in Paris, provided Swearingen with the assurance of repeat business. Despite the many fineries the new Gem Variety Theater had to offer, the second floor continued to feature an assortment of aberrant behaviors to entice the morally depraved. New curtains, fresh paint: same Swearingen, same deviant conduct.[32]

Two months after hiring twenty-four-year-old Inez Sexton, the "Michigan Songstress," to perform at the theater, Swearingen began strongarming her into being a prostitute. Inez had accepted Swearingen's invitation to travel to South Dakota while she was in St. Louis performing with the Oates Opera Company. She had been in Missouri for a short while when the director of the company fired her for the disparaging remarks she made about the company to a local newspaper. It was the middle of the opera season, and all the jobs available with other companies had been filled. Inez was stranded and without prospects. She felt her only option was to sign with the Gem.[33]

The Michigan Songstress made her Deadwood debut on December 30, 1879. She regaled theatergoers with the song "The Last Rose of Summer" and filled the remainder of her time on stage with various arias from Italian operas in which she had starred. The audience was enchanted with her voice, and, by February 1880, she had received more than one proposal of marriage.[34]

The number of men that frequented the Gem in hopes of spending time with Inez was not missed by Swearingen. Like the other entertainers he had persuaded to the area, he wanted the opera star to join his stable of prostitutes and work that job when she wasn't singing. Inez had no intention of becoming a soiled dove, and, until she could come up with a plan to get away from Swearingen, she pretended to be too ill to do anything.[35]

Newspaper reports about her situation were brought to the attention of two benevolent ladies in town, who, like other Deadwood residents,

31

knew how Swearingen acquired the sporting women in his employ. The pair interceded and helped Inez leave the Gem. She moved to a room over a furniture store, and the Samaritans promised to care for her until arrangements could be made to get her back home to Michigan.[36]

Inez was ashamed of the predicament she had gotten herself into with Swearingen, and even though she was physically sound, emotionally she struggled. By May she was feeling well enough to agree to perform at a benefit concert. The proceeds would be used to help her get out of South Dakota. "A number of our good ladies, who understand and appreciate the deplorable situations Miss Inez Sexton has been in since her arrival in the Hills, are getting up a concert for her benefit," the May 26, 1880, edition of the *Black Hills Daily Times* announced.[37]

> *Mrs. Judge Gaffy, and others who are competent to manage a concert without bringing the one whom they desire to assist in debt, have taken hold of the entertainment, and will regale our people with the most charming vocal and instrumental concert ever given in Deadwood.*[38]
>
> *Miss Sexton, who has recovered sufficiently from her long season of "sickness," will also appear and sing several of her enchanting songs. It is calculated to render this the best concert entertainment ever heard in this metropolis.*[39]

The concert was a success. Inez Sexton departed Deadwood on June 9, 1880.[40]

Al Swearingen's brutal, villainous nature and the shameful goings on inside the Gem continually made the front page of Deadwood's various newspapers. A patron named Lena Bruce was the victim of Swearingen's savage behavior in late November 1880. She was watching a group of men gamble, and Swearingen was watching her. Whatever she was doing while bets were being placed violated the rules of the table, and Swearingen interceded with his fists. The assaulted woman reported him to the law, and Swearingen was fined ten dollars for his actions. "A man or thing who will beat a woman is beneath the dignity or notice of his species," an article in the November 27, 1880, edition of the *Black Hills Weekly Times* noted about the incident.[41]

Physical confrontations at the Gem weren't relegated strictly to Swearingen and other aggressive men. Fights between female patrons and the sporting gals who worked at the theater, as well as between the sporting gals themselves, routinely occurred. Ida Clark, a regular Gem theatergoer, was holed up inside one of the curtained box seats watching a variety of musical acts, from Fannie Douglas and Jackson and Mack to Valentine and Morrell and Lizzie Peasley, when Lizzie entered Ida's box seat. Ida struck the song and dance artist in the head with a shot glass, knocking her off her feet. Lizzie struggled for a moment to find her balance and, once she did, lunged at Ida. The two scuffled for several moments with Lizzie "mopping the floor with Ida." A bystander pulled the pair apart from one another, and order was restored.[42]

On May 28, 1880, a fight broke out between two women who served beer at the Gem. Maggie Mitchell, more commonly known as Big Mag, started the brawl when she jerked Lou Desmond's wig off her head. Lou leveled a .22-caliber pistol at Big Mag and fired. The bullet struck her coworker in the hip. The steel corset Big Mag was wearing stopped the bullet from making a full impact. The server was spared severe injury and was treated by a local physician for a flesh wound. Lou was arrested for assault with a deadly weapon and held over for trial.[43]

The case against Lou Desmond was heard in court on June 1, 1880, at ten o'clock in the morning. Lou's attorney treated the jury and witnesses to a detailed history of the internal management of the Gem Variety Theater, including the physical abuse to which the women there were subjected, the rules and regulations that governed the actions of the lady attendants, the choice language used to address one another, and the barbaric methods used to settle disputes. After hearing the sordid and vile conditions Swearingen's employees were expected to adhere to and listening to the prosecution's feeble attempts to argue that Lou Desmond should be convicted, the jury returned a verdict of not guilty.[44]

Neither Maggie Mitchell nor Lou Desmond's reputation suffered from the case as Al Swearingen's did. His character was further sullied by letters sent to the editor of the *Black Hills Daily Times* accusing him of lying about the funds raised from various benefit concerts held at the theater over the years. The money was to be donated to worthy individuals or community causes, but Swearingen had pocketed the contributions. He was never made to address the allegation that he kept donations intended for benevolent purposes but attempts to avoid paying taxes to the city resulted in having to explain his actions to a judge and take responsibility for what was owed.[45]

When the Gem Variety Theater first opened its doors to entertainment-starved Deadwood citizens, much of the publicity the business received centered around the talent featured on stage. By the spring of 1881, however, much of the press focused on the disorderly conduct between the stage acts, the women who served drinks, the women who worked in the bordello, and Swearingen himself.[46]

In May 1881, the *Black Hills Daily Times* reported on another desperate and troubled Gem employee. Kitty Conway was a bartender "who had a smile for those who smiled, and a sigh for those who sighed." She was known to give special attention to men who had a lot of money. Kitty was a pleasure to be around and always seemed happy but looks were deceiving. On May 7, she took a dose of morphine with the intent of killing herself. A doctor was quickly called to the scene, and he pumped the poison out of her stomach. Those who knew her best speculated her heart was broken by a customer she had fallen in love with and was convinced would marry her and take her away from Swearingen and the Gem. When Kitty learned her boyfriend had transferred his affections to another at the business, she didn't want to go on. She recovered physically but was left emotionally scarred.[47]

Swearingen attempted to improve the chaotic atmosphere at the Gem by hiring another ensemble of actors, singers, and dancers he hoped would get along with one another, keep their focus on why they were hired, and stay out of trouble with the law. The new troupe, hired while Swearingen was in New York in late July 1881, arrived in the Black Hills on August 30. The cast of characters changed, but the problems remained the same. The entertainers behaved as badly as their predecessors. Within a month, they were filing complaints against one another for public drunkenness and disorderly conduct.[48]

The out-of-control audience members who came out to see the new cast and new shows at the Gem added to the trouble. The October 17,

1881, edition of the *Black Hills Daily Times* report on the dangerous theatergoers prompted well-mannered customers to do business elsewhere.[49]

> *There is a gang in this city who infest the Gem Variety Theater, who are by no means useful, neither are they ornamental. They do not work, and how they live is a conundrum. On Saturday night a miner named Campbell, from Lead, who had been indulging in the ardent, fell into their clutches and was terribly beaten by them. In self-defense, the miner drew a knife and stabbed Jack Odell in the side, inflicting a slight wound.*[50]

Whatever the Gem Variety Theater might have lacked in ticket sales to the nightly performances, the Gem brothel more than made up for it. Swearingen's prostitutes were always busy, and any difficulties the women had with one another, or the owner of the business, didn't keep customers from regular visits. Occasionally, customers became too attached to the women working for Swearingen and struggled to deal with the idea they spent time with other men. Charley Wilson was one such individual. He was involved with Kitty Klide. The two had met in Chicago in July 1883 and decided to move to Deadwood. Charley worked as a caretaker at a local school, and Kitty served beer at the Gem. The two were seen together often both at the theater and on carriage rides around town.[51]

On November 4, 1883, a smitten Charley arrived at the Gem excited to visit Kitty. He was taken aback to learn she was with another man. Humiliated and depressed, he left Swearingen's place. Charley returned to the business late in the afternoon the following day, carrying a gun. He headed straight for Kitty's room and barged in uninvited. Two shots were heard by the other women on the second floor, and they hurried to the scene. Kitty was lying dead on the floor, and Charley was lying close beside her. She died instantly when the bullet entered her neck and dislocated her vertebrae. Charley then turned the gun on himself and shot a round into his right temple. He didn't die right away. The bullet passed behind the optic nerve and lodged in the left side of his brain. Charley lingered in pain for more than two weeks before succumbing to the injury.

He provided the funds to purchase the ornate coffin in which Kitty was buried and the flowers placed on her grave.[52]

Mayhem and violence were commonplace at the Gem. Customers continued to abuse the sporting girls there, and prostitutes continued to turn on one another. On April 28, 1884, a soiled dove named Gertie took a knife to a coworker named Dutch Ann, slashing her face, head, and neck. Dutch Ann was bleeding profusely when she was rushed to the hospital. Gertie was escorted to jail.[53]

Al Swearingen's sins and the immoral activities taking place at the Gem were the subject of a scathing article in the September 5, 1884, edition of the *Black Hills Daily Times*. A reporter with the newspaper, on hand to witness the arrival of a stagecoach carrying eleven women from Chicago hired to work at the Gem, interviewed the visibly frightened and confused ladies the following day about their journey to Deadwood. During the conversation, they confessed that Swearingen had lied to them about the jobs he wanted them to perform.[54]

"Their demeanor, or at least, the demeanor of a number of them was in strange contrast with their surroundings, being quiet, reserved and calculated to arouse the sympathy of the better class of visitors, who instead of indulging in orgies expected of the place, engaged the girls in conversation, won their confidence to an extent, and listened to disclosures of deceit and upon the part of Swearingen for the purpose of launching innocence and virtue upon a life of shame," the *Black Hills Daily Times* journalist wrote.

It was a sad recital; one to which no one possessed of a spark of manhood could listen without experiencing a sense of indignation, and without offering such assistance as lay within his power to give.[55]

Acting upon the advice of one of the boys whose heart is as big as an ox, one of the sobbing, terrified girls improved a favorable opportunity, slipped through a side door and hastened to the Wentworth house, where she was kindly given shelter. Officer Dunn, apprised of the situation and that Swearingen had locked the girls in the building, consulted with Marshal Tyler, and repaired to the hall where he stood ready to render assistance should any of the inmates desire to leave. The latter, bewildered by the situation, strangers in a strange land, without money, and, as they reasonably believed, without friends, retired to their rooms where, amid tears and lamentations they passed the long hours until morning, when, accepting the help of Marshal Tyler, a number were escorted from the place.[56]

No matter how many times the evils of the Gem and its owner were exposed, business continued to flourish. Comedians, singers, and dancers readily accepted invitations to perform at the theater, and Black Hills patrons purchased tickets to see the shows. Many of those patrons visited the brothel while they were there and purchased drinks for themselves and their friends. Any public comments Swearingen made about the Gem were always about the variety theater and the quality of talent that paraded in and out of the performance center. He and his closest associates tried desperately to depict Swearingen as an honest businessman who had only the best interests of the community in mind. It was an argument used in court after Swearingen was indicted four times for "keeping a disorderly house."[57]

An article that appeared in the September 2, 1887, edition of the *Black Hills Daily Times* went as far as to imply that the reputable entrepreneur was being mistreated by the justice system. "At the recent session of the grand jury in Deadwood an indictment was found against Al Swearingen, charging him with keeping a disorderly house," the report began. "In due course of time the case came up for trial, and Swearingen, in all the dignity of conscious innocence, appeared and entered a plea of not guilty. It was evident that there was a great deal of difficulty in substantiating the charge.[58]

Mr. Swearingen is the proprietor of the Thespian temple commonly known as the Gem Theater, which is advertised in the publications of Deadwood as a model place of amusement, where pleasant and innocent relaxation from the cares and toils of the day may be found seven evenings in each week. It is undoubtedly a case of malicious prosecution, not to say persecution. The jury was probably packed against Mr. Swearingen, as it is found that after having wrestled with the evidence all night long an agreement to honorably acquit him had not been reached.[59]

Ultimately, the jury in the case was unable to agree on a verdict, and the charges against Swearingen were dismissed.[60]

It was business as usual at Al Swearingen's "den of vice" between 1887 and 1894. There were issues with finances, debts that needed to be repaid, another formal accusation for running a house of ill repute, and more Gem employees committing suicide. Eighteen-year-old actress Loudella Perry took her own life on April 5, 1894, by an overdose of morphine. According to the *Weekly Pioneer Times*, she was filled with remorse over the things she had done with the men who visited the establishment. After swallowing the deadly potion, she penned two letters, one to Swearingen and the other to her fiancé in Grand Rapids, Michigan.[61]

My Own Dear Gordon,

When you read this, there will be no more Lou, for I have put an end to myself for reasons you will find out soon enough. I hope you will forgive me and will not hate me when you find out what I have done. Remember, I love you better than my life, and death is easier than to be away from you and not be respected, as I have done something I never meant to do. I hope my mother will have mercy on me, for I meant to lead a better life, but found I could not. So, I shall put an end to all my misery in this world, and I know God will have mercy on me in the next.[62]

The ring you gave me has never been off my finger but once, and that was by accident. When I was wiping my hands, it slipped off, and I put it right on, as it touched my finger all the time. My request is to be buried with it on. Gordon, I must close, as my drugs are taking effect, and I can hardly see. Goodbye forever. Don't drink is my last request. Farewell, Gordon, forever; from one who loved you to the last.[63]

Loudella died sixteen hours after swallowing the poison.[64]

In 1894, Swearingen spent time in court defending himself against another assault charge. His personal life had been plagued with several marriages and divorces and those closest to him, including his attorney, cited his inability to control his temper with his wives and others who challenged him on an issue for his string of arrests.[65]

Swearingen finally met a woman in early 1895 who wouldn't submit to his abuse and returned to him a sample of what he'd subjected his employees and spouses to for many years. On March 18, an inebriated Swearingen burst into Bulah Potter's room at the Gem and demanded attention. Bulah ordered him to leave, and he slapped her. He then picked up a spittoon and tried to throw it at her. With one hand she grabbed his arm to stop him and with the other grabbed his throat and squeezed hard. When Swearingen dropped the spittoon, she tossed him on the bed and clutched his neck with both hands.[66]

"He struggled and assaulted her again when she took a heavy stove shaker, a piece of inch iron about twelve inches long, and wacked Swearingen on the head and he fell to the ground," an article in the March 20, 1895, edition of the *Black Hills Daily Times* explained.

> *The woman was excited and exasperated and went at him again. When she quit, his head showed nine long and deep cuts from which blood flowed freely, and he lay unconscious. A doctor was then called to the room, and Swearingen's injuries were dressed.[67]*
>
> *He regained consciousness in a short time and was able to be about yesterday, though he is a hard looking specimen and has about the toughest looking head we ever saw. This is a very good lesson for the contemptible pup, and everybody is pleased to learn of it.[68]*
>
> *The woman went before Justice Early yesterday and swore out a warrant for Swearingen's arrest on the charge of assault and battery. Swearingen was arrested and appeared before the justice last evening but felt so sore and "weary" that his trial was continued until 2 o'clock this afternoon.[69]*

A fire erupted at the Gem Variety Theater on December 19, 1897, destroying Swearingen's livelihood at the location for the last time. The building was destroyed, and the cause of the fire could not be determined. Swearingen left town shortly after the fire, traveling to the Yukon and Canada. He returned to Deadwood for a brief visit in the fall of 1903. According to the December 31, 1904, edition of the *Rapid City Journal*, Al Swearingen was killed by a switch train in Denver on November 15, 1904. "His body was found lying between a couple of tracks and a wound was found on his head, showing that he had been struck heavily by some large object," a newspaper report noted.[70]

Ellis Albert Swearingen was buried at Forest Cemetery in Oskaloosa, Iowa. He was fifty-nine years old when he died.[71]

2

MADAM ELEANORA DUMONT

HISTORIANS BELIEVE THE SCANDALOUS ELEANORA DUMONT WAS ONE of the first madams to arrive in Deadwood Gulch in 1876. Her time in the Black Hills was brief. She was in her late forties, and much of her life as a prostitute and gambler had already been lived by the time she traveled to Deadwood. "Madame Mustache," as she was also known, stayed in town long enough to fleece a few residents at the faro tables and spend an evening or two with curious men who knew of her reputation. Three years after making her way to the Dakota Territories, Eleanora was living in a gold mining town in California and reminiscing about life in Deadwood.[1]

A pair of miners squinted into the early morning sky as they rode from the gold town of Bodie, California, toward their claim. Shafts of light poked through scattered clouds a few miles ahead on the rocky road. In the near distance, the men spotted what looked like a bundle of clothing lying just out of reach of the sun's tentacles. They speculated that some prospector must have lost his gear riding through the area, but, as they approached the item, it was clear that it was not simply a stray pack. A woman's body lay drawn in a fetal position, dead. The curious miners dismounted and hurried to the unfortunate soul.[2]

The vacant eyes that stared up at the men were those of the famed Eleanora Dumont, the "Blackjack Queen of the Northern Mines." An empty bottle of poison rested near her lifeless frame, and her dusty face was streaked with dried tears. One of the miners covered her with a blanket from his bedroll while the other eyed the vultures circling overhead.

Deadwood 1876, the year Madam Eleanor Dumont arrived in town. COURTESY OF
DEADWOOD HISTORY, INC. ADAMS MUSEUM COLLECTION, DEADWOOD, SD

Misfortune and a broken heart led to the fifty-year-old Dumont's downfall. At one time, she had been the toast of the gold rush and one of the most desirable women in the West. A string of bad luck in love and cards drove her to take her own life.[3]

Eleanora Dumont was born in New Orleans in 1829 and came to San Francisco in the early 1850s. She proudly proclaimed to all who asked that she "did not make the long journey for love of the frontier or to find the man of her dreams." She wanted wealth. "The western heartthrob I'm after is not a man, but that glittery rock lying among the foothills of the Gold Country," she confessed.

Madam Eleanora Dumont, also known as Madam Mustache THE DENVER PUBLIC LIBRARY, WESTERN HISTORY COLLECTION, CALL #C61-5 ART

People of every kind and description poured into San Francisco, bringing tents, building shacks, and sleeping on the ground under blankets draped over poles. Fired with the urge to get into the gold fields and find the mother lode, men leapt from ships. They congregated with the miners who had found gold and come to town to spend it. There was a wild gambling fever in the air. Eleanora capitalized on the fever by working as a dealer at a saloon called the Bella Union. Hardworking prospectors stood in line to lose their chunks of gold to the stunningly beautiful and demure young woman.[4]

Within a few months, Eleanora had earned enough money to invest in her own gambling den. In 1854, she boarded a stage bound for Nevada City, the richest gold town in California, and purchased a vacant storefront to turn into a gaming house. She called herself Madam Dumont and invited thrill seekers to take her on in a game of twenty-one or blackjack.

Her establishment was tastefully decorated and furnished with expensive chairs and settees, carpets, and gas chandeliers. Her resort was open twenty-four hours a day, and patrons were offered free champagne. Even though customers were required to clean off their boots before entering and were ordered to keep their language clean as well, Dumont's place soon became the favorite spot for thirsty gold miners and other characters passing through.[5]

A big part of the attraction was Madam Dumont's superb card playing. She excelled in the game she referred to as *vingt-et-un* or blackjack. The object of the poker game was to accumulate cards with a higher count than that of the dealer but not to exceed twenty-one.

Not everyone approved of a woman operating a gaming house. Dumont was frequently chastised by elite political and social influences in Nevada City. She ignored their remarks and the remarks of the men who lost to her, but she never turned away a customer who insinuated she was a cheat or challenged her to a game. Dutch Carver was a prospector who did just that.[6]

Late one summer evening, the drunken Carver burst into Madam Dumont's house and demanded to see her. "I'm here for a fling at the cards tonight with your lady boss," Carver told one of the scantily attired women who worked at the parlor. He handed the young lady a silver dollar and smiled confidently. "Now, you take this and buy yourself a drink. Come around after I clean out the Madam, and maybe we'll do some celebrating." The woman laughed in Carver's face. "I won't hold my breath," she said.[7]

Eleanora soon appeared at the gambling table dressed in a stylish Garibaldi blouse and skirt. She sat down across from Carver and began shuffling the deck of cards. "What's your preference?" she asked him. Carver laid a wad of money out on the table in front of him. "I don't care," he said. "I've got more than two hundred dollars here. Let's get going now, and I don't want to quit until you've got all my money, or until I've got a considerable amount of yours." She smiled and obligingly began dealing the cards. In a short hour and a half, Dutch Carver had lost his entire bankroll to Madam Dumont.[8]

When the game ended, the gambler stood up and started to leave the saloon. Dumont ordered him to sit down and have a drink on the house.

He took a place at the bar, and the bartender served him a glass of milk. This was a customary course of action at Eleanora's house. All losers had to partake. Madam Dumont believed that "any man silly enough to lose his last cent to a woman deserved a milk diet."[9]

Dumont's reputation as a card sharp spread throughout the foothills of the Gold Country. No one had ever seen a successful woman dealer before. Gaming establishments were dominated by men. Dealing cards and operating a faro table was considered a man's job, and there was not a lot of respectability associated with the position. Eleanora defied convention and proved that the appearance of a beautiful woman behind the gambling table was good business. Curious gamblers from Wyoming to Texas flocked to the club to watch the trim blackjack queen with the nimble fingers shuffle the deck. Rival saloons found it necessary to hire women just to keep up with the competition.

Eleanora's success and beauty attracted many young men. Historical records indicate that several men fell hopelessly in love with the fair Miss Dumont. They proposed marriage and had their hearts broken when she refused. Dell Fallon was one such suitor whose affections she rejected. He popped the question to her one night while sitting across from her at a blackjack table. "Madam Eleanora," he began, "I know I ain't worthy to ask the question. But would you consent to become my wife?"[10]

"My friend," Eleanora gently replied, "I am grateful that you hold me in such high regard. But I am not free to follow the dictates of my heart. I must go alone."[11]

Eleanora could have had men by the score, but her heart was set on just one: editor Waite of the *Nevada Journal*. She adored him and longed for the respectability he offered. Waite never returned her feelings. He did not want to be involved with someone lacking in social standing. Her broken heart over the matter would never really heal. To get through the hurt and rejection, she set her sights on building a bigger gambling casino on the main street of town.[12]

In less than a year after her arrival in the Gold Country, Eleanora had amassed a considerable fortune. Her business continued to grow, and she found she needed to take on a partner to assist with the daily operation of the club. She teamed up with a professional gambler from New York named David Tobin. Together, they opened a larger establishment where Tobin attended the games of faro and keno.

Business was good for a couple of years, but by 1856, the gold mines had stopped producing the precious metal and Eleanora and Tobin decided to dissolve their partnership and move on. Madam Dumont had more than financial reasons for wanting to leave the area. When she found out that editor Waite was sharing his time with a young woman he had planned to marry, she was devastated. Before she left town, she went to see him at the paper. Tears stood in her eyes as she kissed him lightly on the cheek. "I'm leaving Nevada City to forget," she told him. "I hope you have a good life."[13]

Eleanora took her winnings to the rich gold camps of Columbia, California. She set up her table in the hotel, and when profits slowed down, she moved to yet another mining community. She had a reputation for being honest and generous to the losers, and many times she loaned the miners a few dollars to gamble with.

By the time she reached the age of thirty, her good looks had started to fade. The facial hair that grew on her upper lip earned her the nickname "Madame Mustache."

She decided to use the money she had earned to get out of the gambling business altogether and buy a cattle ranch near Carson City, Nevada. The work was hard, and Eleanora knew next to nothing about animals and even less about ranching. She was lonely, out of her element, and desperate. That's when she met Jack McKnight. "I knew when I met him that he was the answer to my prayers," she confessed. "He was just what I needed and at the right time."[14]

Jack McKnight claimed to be a cattle buyer, and he swept Eleanora off her feet. He was actually a scoundrel who made his living off the misfortunes of others. He was handsome, a smooth talker, and very well dressed. The two married shortly after they met. Eleanora married for love. Jack married for money and property. Eleanora trusted him and turned everything she had over to him.[15]

They had been married less than a month when Jack deserted her, taking all her money with him. He had also sold her ranch and left her with all his outstanding debts. Eleanora was crushed.

Alone and destitute, she was forced to return to the mining camps and take up gambling again. She had been away from the blackjack table for more than a year. She wasn't as good a card player as she once was, but she was still fascinating to most. They would come from miles around to hear her stories and to play a hand with the notorious Madam Mustache.[16]

Eleanora took her blackjack game to many backwater towns across the West. She lost more hands than she won, and she began to earn most of her money as a prostitute and started drinking heavily as a way to deal with her tragic life.[17]

At the age of fifty, she settled in the rough and wicked gold mining town of Bodie, California. Bodie had a reputation for violence. Shootings, stabbings, and thefts took place every day. The lady gambler, now frequently intoxicated, set up a blackjack table in one of the saloons there. Professional gamblers took on Eleanora, eventually leaving her penniless. She always had a smile for the men who fleeced her.

One night, after losing yet another hand, she drank down a glass of whiskey and excused herself from the table. The saloon patrons watched her leave the building and stagger off down Main Street. That was the last time Madame Mustache was seen alive. Her body was found on an early September morning in 1879. The *Bodie Daily Free Press* reported her demise in the September 8 evening edition: "A woman named Eleanora Dumont was found dead today about one mile out of town, having committed suicide. She was well known through all the mining camps. Let her many good qualities invoke leniency in criticizing her failings."[18]

Among the personal items found on Eleanora's body was a letter she had written and placed in an envelope for mailing. The envelope, which was addressed to the citizens of Nevada City, was splotched with tearstains. The letter contained a request by Eleanora that she be permitted to be buried in the gold rush town where she opened her first gambling parlor. She wanted to be buried next to her one true love, editor Waite.

Local townspeople were only able to pool enough money together to bury Madame Dumont in the Bodie Cemetery. They gave her a proper burial and refused to let her be laid to rest in the outcast section of the graveyard.

3

MADAM MOLLIE JOHNSON

AMONG THE SPECTATORS ATTENDING THE BASEBALL GAME AT FORT Meade in the Dakota Territory in mid-June 1879 between the Hard Scrabbles and the Never Sweats was brothel owner and operator Mollie Johnson and three of her best employees. All wore burgundy or emerald-green silk taffeta and velvet dresses, and their blonde curls dangled haphazardly from beneath the fancy bonnets on their heads. Mollie and her trio happily passed a bottle of wine around to one another. With each drink, they became more jovial and uninhibited. They giggled, laughed, and tried to engage the intrigued soldiers around them in a loud conversation about the best way to hit the ball. Their unruly behavior drew disapproving looks from sober civilians within their sphere. The women disregarded the angry stares and whispers and continued their celebration. When the game ended, Mollie escorted her girls to a pair of Patton buggies, two-seater horse drawn carriages with canopies. The women clumsily climbed into the vehicles, laughing as they settled in for the ride.[1]

More wine was shared as the least intoxicated of the four women, two in each carriage, took the horses' reins and spurred the animals on their way. The courtesans shouted and waved at onlookers as they passed. The animals hurried along, unsure which path to take as both drivers were too giddy to lead with any confidence.

By the time the carriages reached the open prairie near Crook City between Sturgis and Deadwood, the women were beyond drunk and thoroughly bored with the ride. The road was wide enough for the vehicles to

Deadwood had only been in existence three years when Madam Mollie Johnson arrived on the scene. COURTESY OF DEADWOOD HISTORY, INC. ADAMS MUSEUM COLLECTION, DEADWOOD, SD

travel side by side, and the drivers of both carriages decided it would be fun to engage in a race. The horses sped down the road as the passengers squealed with delight. The scenery on either side became a blur to the inebriated women, and their judgment was further impaired. The vehicles collided, and Mollie and the others were flung from the carriages.[2]

Three of the four women managed to get to their feet. They were dazed and confused, their arms and faces cut and bruised, clothes torn in places, and shoes and bonnets lost somewhere in the brush and rubble. Flora Bell, a popular singer in the Black Hills as well as a soiled dove, was lying unconscious near one of the carriages that was bent and missing a wheel. Mollie rushed to her side, and the others followed. The accident had quickly cleared their heads.

A man passing by noticed the wreckage and spotted the women huddled around Flora. By the time he reached the distressed ladies, Flora had come to and was trying to sit up. The man helped load the injured woman in the carriage that was still drivable and hurried her off to a doctor in Deadwood. Mollie and the others were left behind. They would have to walk back to town.[3]

The women were still on foot when the sun set and the night sky came into plain view. They were tired, hurting, and in tears when three well-known men from Deadwood riding broncos met them on the road. After Mollie explained to them what had happened, the trio was invited to take a seat behind the men in their saddles and ride home.[4]

It was past two in the morning when the women and their escorts arrived in Deadwood. Still shaken and disheveled, Mollie and her girls returned to the bordello after promising the men to repay their kindness the following evening.[5]

Madam Mollie Johnson was born in Alabama in 1853. According to the 1880 census, her parents were from County Cork, Ireland, and she was a widow. She was twenty-five years old when she opened her house of ill repute in Deadwood on Sherman Street. Prior to deciding to operate a brothel, she agreed to marry an actor named Lew Spencer.[6] He frequently played at the Bella Union Theater in town and was more than a fair singer and comedian. Not long after the two were wed, Spencer left for Denver without Mollie. While in Colorado, Lew married another woman whom he shot in a fit of jealous rage. The woman lived, and Spencer was arrested for the crime. After serving a jail sentence, he returned to the stage.[7]

Mollie was known as the "Queen of the Blondes." All the women who worked for her had golden hair and pleasing figures. In addition to being prostitutes, they were also entertainers. Some were balladists, and some were dancers. Mollie was a shadow dancer. She performed wearing little or no clothing, but patrons could only see her shadow projected on a screen by a bright light. Advertisements to attend parties in which Mollie would appear were posted regularly in newspapers throughout the Black Hills, and people flocked to the bordello to see her.[8]

Men hoping to keep their moral integrity intact went out of their way to avoid walking past Mollie's business for fear of being lured inside. A

Ladies at a bordello in the Black Hills AUTHOR'S COLLECTION

reporter for the *Black Hills Daily Times* wrote about his struggle to resist the temptations at Mollie's house in August 1879. The man was taking a leisurely stroll on a hot summer's night when he found himself on the street leading to the madam's place.[9]

> *At the dead of night when all nature is hushed asleep, this reporter is frequently regaled, while on his way home, by the gentle cadence of sweet songs which floats out upon the stillness of the gulch like the silvery horns of Elfland faintly blowing. Vocal music, wherever heard or by whatever produced, is entrancing to this sinner. Hence the aforesaid sounds are sure to arrest his step at the corner and compel him to lend his ear to the mellifluent melody which steals out from Molly Johnson's Harem.*[10]
>
> *But he does not draw any nearer, for he knows that where the sirens dwell you linger. That their songs are death. . . . To avoid destruction he travels on, disgusted with himself because his virtuous life possesses such a skeleton of fun, yet wonders that such a voluptuous harmony is tolerated by the divine muse of song to leave such a bad place.*[11]

Mollie didn't consider her business comparable to other bordellos. Hers was not a saloon with upstairs rooms or a hurdy-gurdy with makeshift cribs behind the building. Mollie's house was high-class in her estimation, and she wasn't shy about letting women who worked in those inferior locations know it. She often rented a large open carriage for herself and her employees to ride through town in and insult the "less handsome and prosperous" soiled doves.[12]

Mollie cared deeply for the women at her house. She made sure they were healthy, properly clothed, and protected. In the fall of 1879, one of Mollie's best girls, Josephine Willard, more commonly known as Jennie Phillips, died after being ill for more than a month. The madam was brokenhearted over the loss. On July 6, Jennie and the other sporting women in Mollie's employ had taken a ride in the country and come across a wild cat that had been chained to a tree by the owner of a tollgate.[13] Enchanted by the animal, Jennie scooped it up in her arms and stroked its neck. She then tried to kiss the animal, and it turned on her and bit her lip. She started feeling ill shortly after the incident.[14]

"During her brief sickness she had every attention that money, and the hands of her erring sisters could extend," a report in the September 26, 1879, edition of the *Black Hills Daily Times* noted about Jennie's passing. "She was the only child of wealthy parents now residing in Chicago, where her father is a leading saddlery hardware merchant and lives in luxury. What induced her to leave such a home and live an abandoned life is one of the mysteries that can only be conjectured."[15]

Mollie was still mourning Jennie's passing when a fire erupted in town. Her brothel was one of many buildings consumed by the flames that nearly destroyed Deadwood in September 1879. Firefighters encouraged Mollie to vacate her home before the blaze overtook the structure, but she refused to leave until Jennie's body, lying in a coffin in the parlor, was safely removed. The coffin was quickly taken out of the building and transported to another location. Jennie was buried the next day at Mount Moriah Cemetery.[16]

Mollie paid $7,000 to build a new house on the ashes where her old one once stood. The "Queen of Blondes" was back in business by Christmas and hosting holiday parties in which she charged customers two dollars to attend. Mollie prided herself on supporting the community. She routinely donated money to civic organizations, but particularly so during the holidays. She gave money to churches to buy presents for needy children, to the city founders for July 4 celebrations, meals, and clothing for the poor, and books for schools.[17]

Mollie expected her girls to behave themselves in public; if they couldn't, they should at least not get caught. One of the women working for the madam and traveling by train from Omaha to the Black Hills proved unable to fulfill either request. When the young prostitute boarded the train, she spoke with some of the passengers and told them she was enroute to meet her fiancé. During the trip, she befriended a man who showed more than a passing interest in her. Their flirtatious actions were deemed scandalous by their fellow travelers, and an article about the affair made the February 15, 1880, edition of the *Weekly Pioneer Times*.[18]

The passengers on No. 3 train from the East that passed through Cheyenne yesterday were both amused and incensed at the conduct of a young lady and a male passenger. The two got aboard the sleeper at Omaha and were located at either end of the car. They were total strangers until they met upon the train.[19]

The young lady told a female passenger early in the day that she was on her way to Deadwood to get married to a young man who had left the East two years ago and had since acquired wealth.[20]

She was a very pretty and fascinating creature, and she soon "mashed" the young man aforesaid, who started a flirtation. The result was that the two were soon together in her seat playing at cards. The passengers, knowing that they were strangers, kept an eye upon all their movements. The young man was over-agreeable. He bought his newly made friend all the knick-knacks vended by the trainman and was "just ever so kind."[21]

They frequently indulged in very confidential whisperings and appeared delighted over the result. They billed and cooed and were seemingly as happy as a newly wedded couple, and to all appearances the young woman had entirely forgotten about her betrothed away up in Deadwood.

To the astonishment of the passengers, the young lady had the por-
ter prepare her bunk early in the evening. It was in the rear of the car,
but the passengers were intent on keeping posted as to events.[22]

The young man took his own seat in front, and sat quietly until
the next station was reached, when he got out, going out at the front
of the car. He was not seen to enter again upon the train start-
ing and in fact was remarked as being very singular, for he was
known to be a through passenger, having boasted of his possessions
in Nevada.

The more he didn't show up the more curious his fellow-passengers
became. One man finally went searching through the entire train but
failed to see him. Finally, an elderly lady whispered something to her
husband, the husband called a caucus of the male passengers, and the
result was that a committee of one was appointed to call in the conduc-
tor and porter. Those two officials arrived and were informed of the
suspicions of the party.[23]

The conductor knocked at the bunk of the aforesaid young lady,
and, after a scene that will not be described here, a young man clad
in red and white flannel bounced on the floor in his stocking feet and,
wonderfully strange, it was the same young man who had been so
closely attached to the young lady during the afternoon.[24]

The young man displayed a great amount of cheek, and coolly
dressed himself, defying the taunts of the passengers and threatening to
spill gore.[25] *He ordered his bunk let down and went to bed, muttering*
curses against those who had "got him into trouble."

In the morning, the expectant bride got off at Sidney, being des-
tined for the Black Hills, and the young man went into the smoking
car, where his exploit of the previous night was unknown.[26]

The February 17, 1880, edition of Deadwood's newspaper, the *Black Hills Daily Times,* called the sleeping car exploit demoralizing. Although Mollie would have preferred her employee to have been a bit more discrete, the publicity did not have an adverse effect on her business. Indeed, patrons flocked to the Sidney stage office in Deadwood whenever news that Mollie had hired a bevy of new blond beauties to work for her. The women received enthusiastic greetings, and, like the Pied Piper, men followed the madam to her profitable bordello to spend the evening.[27]

Occasionally, one of Mollie's girls, with hopes of falling in love and leaving the business, got lucky. Annie Hizer, known to customers as Little Buttercup, met Dr. C. W. Meyer, a leading physician in the Black Hills, at Mollie's place, and the couple knew instantly they couldn't live without the other. Annie and Dr. Meyer were married on March 7, 1880, at the Cooley and Doherty Opera House. Among those who attended the ceremony were Deadwood's city officials, military officers from nearby Fort Meade, family members from Virginia and New Jersey, and newspaper editors. Mollie and several of Annie's coworkers served as the matron of honor and bridesmaids.[28]

Unlike other brothel owners in the area, Mollie was never arrested or fined for operating a house of ill repute. That did not mean she wasn't ever in court during her time in Deadwood. In the spring of 1880, Mollie sold a diamond ring and several bottles of wine to a Mrs. Hattie Harnett who worked at the local assay office. The details of the sale are lacking, but the court records indicate that Mollie never received payment for the goods. She sued Hattie for the money in early April. The trial was held in May, and the jury ruled in Mollie's favor. Hattie, however, did not have the money to pay the plaintiff. The judge ordered Hattie to sell one of the parcels of land she owned in Deadwood to fulfill the obligation.[29]

Mollie was also in court during that time filing a complaint against Charlie Stacy who was a friend of bordello competitor Al Swearingen. Stacy was arrested for drunk and disorderly conduct at Mollie's house and placed under $150 bond. The case against him was dismissed because Mollie failed to get to court in time to testify against him. Four months after the incident with Stacy, Mollie swore out a complaint against a known thief named William Ward. Ward had assaulted one of Mollie's girls and she had him arrested. He was ordered to pay a fifteen dollar fine.[30]

The South Deadwood Hose Company responded to a fire at Mollie's place at seven o'clock in the evening in late November 1880. The fire started in a pile of wood stacked behind a stove in one of the sporting women's rooms. Unlike the inferno that swept through Deadwood and destroyed Mollie's house the year prior, this flare-up was quickly extinguished. According to an article in the November 20, 1880, edition of the *Black Hills Weekly Times*, "A few pails full of water effectively squelched it, and it was lucky it did, as in a few moments more the house would have been deluged with water."[31]

It was the second time the fire department had been called to Mollie's house in a week. A chimney fire had brought the hose company to the scene a few days earlier. Mollie and her employees were then advised to be more careful. The firefighters warned them against building a big fire and then leaving the room without being sure that everything was safe.

Mollie seldom had any issues with the women who worked for her. Anna Bennett was the rare exception. The soiled dove brought a charge of theft against the madam in January 1881. Anna claimed that Mollie and two other women employed at the house stole assorted items from her room, including two of her silk dresses. The matter was eventually settled in court with Mollie being made to reimburse Anna for the stolen items.[32]

By 1881, Mollie had expanded her empire and was operating a bordello in Leadville, Colorado, as well as the house in Deadwood. In the beginning, it seemed the brothel would be as successful and void of problems with the law as her house in the Black Hills, but trouble arose weeks after opening her doors.

"Early on the morning of the second, the house of ill repute presided over by Mollie Johnson, on State Street, was the scene of a stabbing affray, which may yet result in a cruel and cold-blooded murder," the February 10, 1881, edition of the *Black Hills Daily Times* reported.

It seems that about midnight a man named Aherne entered the place and treated the women to beer. While talking with another man, a stranger came in and after drinking with the party was requested to "set them up" himself. He declined to do this and at the same time began to heap abuse upon those present.[33]

Aherne, to whom he applied the epithet, son of a _____, jumped up to eject him from the house, the ruffian suddenly drew a knife and stabbed him twice, once in the breast and once behind the back. The would-be murderer upon this fled, and the victim sank to the floor unconscious. Aid was at once summoned, and the wounded man's injuries dressed. He was removed to the hospital today, and his death and recovery are in equal balance. There is no clue to the assassin, and from all appearances he seems to be a stranger.[34]

To detract from the tragedy in Colorado, Mollie hosted a series of elaborate balls. Only the most respected clients were invited to attend. The well-mannered guests were treated to several shadow dance numbers by Mollie's "dazzling galaxy of beauties." The notion that respectable men who did business at Mollie's place would function as appropriately during regular visits to the house as they did during the fancy parties was inaccurate. Bank manager Coney Hoffman and lumber yard owner James E. Witherspoon had too much to drink at the ball and decided to cause trouble. They went into the street and began throwing rocks at the bordello, breaking several windows. Mollie had the men arrested and banned from coming near her property again.[35]

Mollie's ability to manage the women who worked for her and keep them in line prompted the mothers of two unruly teens to reach out to her for help. An article in the December 16, 1881, edition of the *Black Hills Daily Times* described the circumstances surrounding the desperate mother's appeal to the tough madam. The girls, referred to as Miss Pettijohn and Miss Woodall, had been arrested in Central City for attempting to solicit money from men in exchange for sexual favors. After the teenagers were released on bail, their mothers escorted them to Mollie's house where the pair were to reside for a time.[36]

"In justice to Madam Mollie, we must say that she would never be a party to the ruin of a young girl," the *Black Hills Daily Times* article noted.

On the contrary, it is recorded to her credit she has assisted foolish girls by money and advice to lead a pure and virtuous life, but these young dames were all beyond aid. They were bad eggs, so bad that nothing could spoil them, and she accepted them as boarders. We are not so certain, but this change is a benefit all around. They are now publicly known for what they are, therefore, they cannot contaminate other girls.[37]

At Madam Mollie's house they will have to preserve external decency in speech and action. We cannot congratulate Miss Pettijohn or Miss Woodall on their new departure, but we hope now that they are in a house, they will forget the brutal indecency they learned and practiced on the streets.[38]

Mollie Johnson came and went from Deadwood often in 1882. The last mention of the madam appeared in the local newspapers in January 1883, announcing her departure from the area. Whether she moved on to open brothels in other boomtowns is unknown.

Madam Dora DuFran COURTESY OF DEADWOOD HISTORY, INC. ADAMS MUSEUM COLLEC-
TION, DEADWOOD, SD

4

MADAM DORA DUFRAN

JUDGE HAROLD R. HANLEY HAMMERED THE STRIKING BLOCK WITH HIS gavel after announcing the verdict the jury had rendered against one of the Black Hills most well-known madams, Dora DuFran. It was 1928, and the Rapid City, South Dakota, courtroom was filled with curious onlookers eager to learn the specifics in the case against the brothel owner brought by a Hot Springs resident named Alice Olson. The lawyers for both women, along with the other official participants, had been careful not to make public the details that prompted the lawsuit. The jury knew all that was needed to decide the matter, but the gallery only heard the general statements made by the counsel. Sometime prior to the hearing, Dora allegedly performed an unwanted illegal procedure on Olson that left her incapable of having children. Olson sued Dora for $10,500. Dora hadn't had any formal training in medicine but, in her line of work, had acquired the basic skills in treating cuts, infections, and midwifery. Dora helped unwed women deliver their babies and performed abortions as well.[1]

Dora, a sixty-year-old, stout, curvy woman, dressed in an off-white taffeta dress trimmed with fur and a matching hat adorned with massive feathers, exchanged a few words with her attorney after the judge informed her the jury found in Olson's favor. Dora's lawyer had argued that the operation she performed on the plaintiff had been necessary because Olson was suffering from a "morbid disease." The jury believed Dora had acted irresponsibly and awarded Olson $3,000. Dora didn't agree with the decision and felt certain her attorney would appeal the case.[2]

By January 1932, the Olson-DuFran case was still being fought in the courts. The appeal had been denied, and Dora had been ordered to pay the predetermined amount. She had been slow in getting Olson the money she was due because she didn't agree with the court's ruling, and a motion had been filed to keep Dora from selling certain property until the judgment had been honored. It would take another two years before the situation would be resolved. Dora believed she did nothing wrong and that paying Olson anything would be an admission of guilt.[3]

Dora DuFran was a stubborn and determined woman. Born Amy Helen Dorothea Bolshaw in England on November 16, 1868, she had immigrated to America with her parents, John and Isabella, in 1870. The Bolshaws lived in Bloomfield, New Jersey, before moving to Lincoln, Nebraska. John was a butcher and Isabella a housewife who cared for Amy and her other children. Amy left home at the age of seventeen, and her travels took her to Rapid City. Like many young, unattached women in the rugged West, she found work entertaining cowboys and prospectors at a dance hall. Dora drifted from Rapid City to Deadwood where she met her husband, Black Hills pioneer Joseph DuFran. In addition to operating a freight hauling business, he was also a gambler. He and Dora were married in 1887. The ambitious couple combined their talents for business and entertaining and opened a string of brothels. The DuFran's had houses in Lead, Rapid City, Belle Fourche, and Deadwood.[4]

Unlike competitors such as Al Swearingen, Dora treated her employees kindly, made sure their work environment was safe and clean, and that they were well paid. A maid was hired to take care of their laundry and make their beds, a handyman was hired to maintain the house, and cooks were hired to provide the women with regular meals. One of the cooks employed to make breakfast, lunch, and dinner was Calamity Jane. The Deadwood celebrity worked at Dora's house in 1903 and was paid eight dollars a week.[5]

For a time, the DuFran's bawdy house in Belle Fourche was the most profitable of their businesses. Cowboys on cattle drives frequented the place known as "Diddlin' Dora's," spending money on liquor and for an evening with one of the soiled doves. Advertisements Dora created to promote the brothel informed patrons that it was the perfect destination for "dining, drinking, and dancing." She went so far to claim the house was "a place where you can bring your mother." Regular customers confessed they wouldn't want their mothers to know they had visited the bordello, let alone take them along when they stopped by.[6]

The DuFran's good fortune with the Belle Fourche bordello ended abruptly in the spring of 1906 when a disgruntled employee set fire to the two-story home on April 6. According to the April 7, 1906, edition of the *Daily Deadwood Pioneer Times*, there were nearly a dozen men and women in the house at the time the fire was discovered. Dora, along with the prostitutes and their customers, were forced to make a hasty exit into the street in their night clothes.[7]

The fire was discovered shortly after 3 o'clock in the morning by someone who turned in an alarm and notified the occupants of the house. It was found that a shed in back of the house where some coal oil is kept had been set afire, apparently with a match, and the flames soon spread to the dwelling.[8]

The fire department responded quickly and, after considerable hard work, managed to extinguish the flames. . . . Most of the interior of the house was destroyed. A man by the name of Redding was arrested in Belle Fourche the day after the incident and charged with setting the house on fire. Redding was formerly employed there and was discharged a few days ago. It is said that he declared he would get even with [the owner of] the house. He is also said to have been arrested once before on a charge of arson.[9]

Dora's house of ill repute and its furnishings were covered by insurance; in time the DuFrans rebuilt the Belle Fourche business, and customers returned in droves. Although Dora's treatment of the women who worked for her was decent and fair and her interaction with Black Hills residents was courteous and respectful, many law-abiding citizens found her profession contemptable. As such, she was subject to the same consequences for running a brothel as reprehensible characters such as Al Swearingen. Dora was arrested and fined twice in 1907 for "keeping a disorderly house."[10]

The brothel Dora operated in the red-light section of Rapid City called Coney Island was not only one of her most successful ventures, but also the one with the most complaints. On February 2, 1907, Dora was in court to answer a charge for running a house of prostitution in Rapid City and fined twenty dollars. Ten months later, the business was under scrutiny again. Members of the clergy, determined to rid the city of drunks and debauchery, waged war against Dora. They petitioned the court to have the den of iniquity closed.[11]

According to the December 31, 1907, edition of the *Rapid City Journal*, "Keeping a house of prostitution is a serious offense under the laws of this state, and punishable with imprisonment." This time Dora paid a $300 fine, and business continued as usual. She had another encounter with the law in early 1908 involving the sale of liquor without a license. Another hefty fine was imposed, but daily visits to brothels remained uninterrupted. When the reverends that spearheaded the attempt to stop the moral depravity realized the authorities would not shut the madam's busy house down, they organized a series of revivals. Dora and the sporting girls at her house were invited to attend.[12]

Dora's life was forever changed on August 3, 1908, when her husband passed away at the hospital in Hot Springs after suffering for six weeks with kidney issues. The forty-seven-year-old man was laid to rest at Mount Moriah Cemetery in Deadwood. Dora dealt with her loss by focusing on her job, her enterprises, and the two children she and Joseph shared.[13]

Business at the Coney Island brothel seldom slowed. Men visited Dora's place at all hours of the day and night, during snowstorms or torrential downpours. Such was the case in 1909. Thunderstorms flooded streets, railroads, and mines.[14] Bridges, like the one near Dora's creek bottom resort, were washed out. The occupants were forced to remain with the soiled doves until the waters receded enough and they could return home. According to historian and author Robert Casey,

> There were nearly fifty women [wives of the men trapped at Dora's place] along the bank, although probably no more than half that number were personally interested in the proceedings. And all of them

*carried weapons of some sort or other, including wooden rolling pins
which I had believed to be the special property of uninspired cartoon-
ists. The greater number of the amazons carried umbrellas which they
kept tightly rolled. Nobody gave a thought to what implements Dora's
men who came to dinner might present in defense. It was too obvious that they were going to return to the mainland just as they were,
without one plea.*[15]

Madam DuFran's house of ill fame in Lead made the front page of the
Black Hills Weekly Journal in late July 1913 when two of the women working for her battled over a customer. At midnight, Big Jess, an employee at
the brothel, charged into the room of coworker Jessie Taylor and shot a
man named Thomas Jones. The bullet was fired from a .32-caliber revolver
and caught Jones on the underside of the left hand, cutting the fleshy part
of the thumb and passing through the palm and exiting near the little
finger.[16]

Big Jess was arrested and taken to jail, and a local physician took care
of Jones's wound and sent him home. Jones was not the target Big Jess
wanted to shoot; he just happened to be near the woman who was the
target. Big Jess's aim was poor, and Jones got the bullet intended for her
rival.[17]

On rare occasions some of the men who visited Dora's houses were
arrested for solicitation. On November 7, 1913, Dora and Bessie Wright,
one of the girls who worked at the Lead brothel, were called to court to
testify in the cast against Arthur Olsen. Dora had warned Olsen to keep
away from her business, but he had refused. After breaking into Bessie's
room, police were called to remove the man from the premises.[18]

When he was asked why he didn't stay away from the resort, Olsen
said that he could not understand why he should be made an example
of when there were others who stopped by just as often without being
harassed. Both Dora and Bessie explained to the jury that Olsen was not
always sober during his visits and that his behavior was unruly. Olsen
disagreed. He told the jury that he wasn't a lush and maintained a job.
He noted that he "remained away from Dora's house for three weeks after
being warned, but that lately he had frequented the place as often as three

times a week and was then taken into custody." Olsen claimed that no one could swear he was seen under the influence of liquor and that his conduct had never been noisy or objectionable in any way. He asked for fair treatment and called a former employer to the stand who told the court that he had always secured the services of Olsen whenever he needed him, and that the young man was always willing to work and had never been an idler.[19]

The jury left the court at five o'clock to deliberate and came in two hours later with a verdict of guilty with recommendations for leniency. Olsen was sentenced to three months imprisonment. That sentence was suspended for good behavior.[20]

Arthur Olsen wasn't the only frequent patron at Dora's resort in Lead who caused trouble. On December 23, 1913, Charles Lashley was arrested for assaulting one of the girls named Cleo Clark. Lashley was taken into custody and, after spending the night in jail, was made to pay a ten dollar fine for his actions.[21]

Between 1914 and 1918, Dora took care of her son and daughter and managed her various houses without incident. That was due in part to the strict rule of sobriety to which she insisted her staff adhere. The prostitutes who worked for her were not allowed to drink, but patrons were welcome to partake. Dora sold beer for one dollar a glass. The price was high, but her business never lacked for customers because of the cost.[22]

The Spanish influenza pandemic of 1918 struck the Black Hills hard. The need for volunteer nurses to assist doctors in caring for flu victims was great. Dora decided to close her brothels and dedicate herself to assisting those who contracted the disease. She offered her services to Rapid City doctor F. G. Gilbert and immediately started calling on patients too sick to leave their homes to visit the doctor. Dora received no pay for her services and often used her own money to purchase food, medicine, and bedding for the suffering. Dr. Gilbert was moved by Dora's generosity and referred to her as a "natural nurse."[23]

When the epidemic subsided, Dora converted her Coney Island house into a makeshift hospital and catered to the hungry and destitute. She didn't escape the ordeal without her own health struggles. The February 8, 1920, edition of the *Rapid City Journal* noted that "Mrs. DuFran has done

Calamity Jane worked for Dora DuFran and the two became good friends. In 1932, Dora wrote a book about the Western legend entitled *Low Down on Calamity Jane*. COURTESY OF DEADWOOD HISTORY, INC. ADAMS MUSEUM COLLECTION, DEADWOOD, SD

such good work all the past year nursing the sick of every description that it is hoped she will have the best care and get along nicely."[24]

Dora recovered and returned to her life in Rapid City where her benevolence extended to providing food and clothing to the poor. Dora is mentioned several times in the *Rapid City Journal* as having contributed to the general fund at supermarkets so the poor could go and shop.[25]

In 1932, Dora decided to author a book about her time with Calamity Jane. The two became well acquainted while Jane was working for Dora, and the former madam wanted to share what she knew about the legendary woman. The book entitled *Low Down on Calamity Jane* was self-published and released under Dora's pseudonym, D. Dee.[26]

Dora attended the 1933 World's Fair in Chicago and set up a table in the South Dakota booth where she sold copies of her book for fifty cents. Historians note that Dora was so disappointed over poor sales of the title that she burned the stock she had printed when she returned home.[27]

Dora DuFran's life ended on August 5, 1934. She died from heart trouble at her home in Rapid City. Local newspapers referred to her as an "early Black Hill's character" and praised her many charitable deeds. Dora was laid to rest beside her husband at Mount Moriah Cemetery. She was sixty-five years old at the time of her death.[28]

5

MADAM ALICE IVERS

A STEADY STREAM OF MINERS, RANCHERS, AND COWHANDS FILTERED IN and out of the Saloon No. 10 in Deadwood. An inexperienced musician playing an out-of-tune accordion squeezed out a familiar melody, ushering the pleasure seekers inside. Burlap curtains were pulled over the dusty windows, and fans that hung down from the ceiling turned lazily.[1]

A distressed mahogany bar stood alongside one wall of the business, and behind it was a surly-looking bartender. He was splashing amber liquid into glasses as fast as he could. A row of tables and chairs occupied the area opposite the bar, every seat was filled with a card player. Among the male gamblers was one woman; everyone called her "Poker Alice."

She was an alarming beauty, fair-skinned and slim. She had one eye on the cards she was dealing and another on the men at the game two tables down.

Warren G. Tubbs was studying the cards in his hand so intently he didn't notice the hulk of a man next to him get up and walk around behind him. The huge man with massive shoulders and ham-like hands that hung low to his sides peered over Tubbs's shoulder and scowled down at the mountain of chips before him. Alice's intensely blue eyes carefully watched the brute's actions. He casually reached back at his belt and produced a sharp knife from the leather sheath hanging off his waist. Just as he was about to plunge the weapon into Tubbs's back, a gunshot rang out.[2]

A sick look filled the man's face, and the frivolity in the saloon came to a halt. He slowly dropped the knife. Before dropping to his knees, he

Madam Alice Ivers, also known as Poker Alice SOUTH DAKOTA STATE HISTORICAL SOCI-ETY, SOUTH DAKOTA DIGITAL ARCHIVES, 2008-07-07-034

turned in the direction from which the bullet had come. Alice stared back at him, her .38-pistol pointed at his head. The man fell face-first onto the floor. His dead body was quickly removed to make way for another player. In a matter of minutes, the action inside the tavern returned to normal. Tubbs caught Alice's gaze and grinned. He nodded to her and waggled his fingers in a kind of salute. She smiled slightly and wholly turned her attention back to the poker game in front of her.

Alice Ivers never sat down to play poker without holding at least one gun. She generally carried a pistol in her dress pocket, and often she also had a backup weapon in her purse. The frontier was rough and wild, and wearing a gun, particularly while playing cards, was a matter of survival. It was a habit for Poker Alice.[3]

She was born on February 17, 1851, in Sudbury, Devonshire, England. Alice's father, whom some historians indicate was a teacher, while

Madam Alice Ivers engages in a game of poker with friends while her employees are busy in another part of the brothel. SOUTH DAKOTA STATE HISTORICAL SOCIETY, SOUTH DAKOTA DIGITAL ARCHIVES, 2008-07-07-035

others maintain he was a lawyer, brought his wife and family to the United States in 1863. They settled first in Virginia and later moved to Fort Meade, South Dakota.[4]

Like most people at the time, the Iverses were lured west by gold. No matter what gold rush town she was living in, Alice always attended school. She was a bright young girl who excelled in math. The yellow-haired, precocious child quickly grew into a handsome woman, attracting the attention of every eligible bachelor in the area. Frank Duffield, a mining engineer, won her heart and hand. After the two married, he escorted his bride to Lake City, where he was employed. The southwestern Colorado silver camp was an unrefined, isolated location with little to offer in terms of entertainment.[5]

Apart from watching the card sharps and high-hatted gamblers make a fortune off the luckless miners, there was nothing but work to occupy time.

Bored with life as a simple homemaker and undaunted by convention, Alice visited the gambling parlors. Her husband and his friends taught her how to play a variety of poker games and in no time she became an exceptional player. The fact that she was a mathematical genius added tremendously to her talent.[6]

Most every night Alice was seated at the faro table of the Gold Dust Gambling House, dealing cards, and challenging fast-talking thrill seekers to "put their money into circulation." She won most of the hands she played, whether it was five-card draw, faro, or blackjack. Her days of gambling for pleasure alone ended when Frank was killed in a mining accident. Left with no viable means of support, Alice decided to turn her hobby into a profession.[7]

Some well-known gamblers, like Jack "Lucky" Hardesty, were not as accepting of a woman card sharp as others. He made his thoughts on the subject plainly known one evening when he sat down at a faro table and glanced across the green felt at Alice. He refused to play against her, insisting that faro was a man's game.[8]

Alice didn't shy away from the verbal assault. She calmly conveyed her intention to remain at the table until he dealt her a hand. Hardesty eventually gave in, but before he let her have any cards, he warned her not to cry when she lost to him. Poker Alice simply grinned.

At the end of the night, Hardesty was out everything. Alice had won more than $1,500 off him and the other men who wagered on the game. Curious onlookers were reported to have remarked that he had "lost his money like he had a hole in his pocket as big as a stove pipe." Hardesty attributed Alice's numerous wins to luck alone.[9]

Alice took that so-called luck from Colorado to other gambling spots in Arizona, Oklahoma, Kansas, Texas, New Mexico, and South Dakota. Along the way, the fashionable beauty developed a habit of smoking cigars and a taste for alcohol. Wherever the stakes were high, the whiskey smooth, and the smokes free, that's where Alice would be. She generally said nothing if she won, but if she lost a hand, she'd blurt out, "G-damn it!"

The name Poker Alice meant increased business for gaming houses. People flocked to see the highly skilled poker player "packing a heavy load of luck" and puffing on a thin black stogie. Warren G. Tubbs was one of the many who came to see Alice play cards. Warren was a house painter and part-time gambler.[10] He was captivated by her so much so, he didn't mind losing a hand or two to her. She found him equally charming, and after a brief courtship the pair married.[11]

Alice was the better card player of the two and was the primary financial supporter for the family. Tubbs continued with his painting business but would not give up the game entirely. The couple spent many evenings playing poker at the same parlor. Whatever Warren lost Alice made up for in substantial winnings. The average night's win for her was more than $200.

Alice's reputation preceded her. To every town the pair traveled, she was offered twenty-five dollars a night, plus a portion of her winnings, to act as dealer for the gaming parlor. Alice and Warren were bringing in substantial amounts of money and spending just as much. Alice made frequent visits to New York where she would purchase the finest clothes and jewels, attend several theatrical performances and musicals, and lavish her friends with expensive gifts. When the cash ran out, she would return to her husband and her cards and begin rebuilding her bank.[12]

Warren drank to excess and frequently started fights. Poker Alice was very protective of her husband and got him out of trouble many times, ending any squabble that threatened his life. Sober, Warren might have been faster on the draw against an offended cowhand. Alice was the better shot most of the time. Her father had taught her how to shoot using his Starr Army .44-revolver. By the age of twelve, she was as fast and accurate with the weapon as any boy her age. When she got older and there were lulls between poker games, Alice would practice her marksmanship by shooting knobs off the frames of pictures hanging on the walls. Her proficiency with a gun was proof to anyone who thought of crossing her or Warren that she could handle herself.[13]

In 1874, Warren and Alice made their way to New Mexico. They had heard that the money to be made at the poker tables in Silver City were some of the richest in the country. Within hours after their arrival, Alice joined a faro game. Hand after hand she raked in piles of chips. Saloon patrons pressed in around the game to watch the brilliant blonde win again and again. Before the sun rose the following morning, Alice had broken the bank and added to her holdings an estimated $150,000.[14]

Alice and Warren followed the gold rush riches to the town of Deadwood, South Dakota. There, they hoped to continue increasing their winnings. Her expert card playing and beautiful East Coast gowns brought gamblers to her table. Residents referred to her as the "Faro Queen of Deadwood."[15]

Whenever Wild Bill Hickok was around, he liked to play against the queen. In fact, he had invited her to sit in on a hand with him on August 2, 1876, the day Jack McCall shot and killed the legendary Western character. Alice had declined, stating that she had already committed to another game. When she heard he'd been killed, she raced to the scene. Hickok was sprawled out on the floor, and McCall was running for his life. Looking down at her friend's body, she sadly said, "Poor Wild Bill. He was sitting where I would have been if I'd played with him."[16]

In 1910, Alice and Warren celebrated thirty-four years of marriage. Together, they had won and lost a fortune, bought, and sold several ranches in Colorado and South Dakota, and raised seven children. In the winter of that year, Warren contracted pneumonia and died. Alice remarried less than a year later. Her new husband was an obnoxious drunk named George Huckert. Huckert died on their third wedding anniversary.[17]

At this point in her long life, Poker Alice had rid herself of the fashionable dress she once subscribed to and took to wearing khaki skirts, men's shirts, and an old campaign hat. Her beauty had all but faded, and her hair had turned silver. The only thing that remained of the Alice of old was her habit of smoking cigars.[18]

After moving back and forth from Deadwood to Rapid City and back again, Poker Alice left Deadwood for good in 1913. She relocated to Sturgis, South Dakota, and bought a home a few miles from Fort Meade. She also purchased a profitable "entertainment" business, one that attracted hordes of soldiers stationed at the post. In addition to female companionship, she also sold bootleg whiskey. There were times in her career as madam that the combination proved deadly.[19]

It was a warm mid-July evening in 1913 when twenty-six-year-old Private Fred Koetzle began hurling rocks at Poker Alice Tubb's brothel in Sturgis, eventually shattering the upstairs windows. Koetzle and

Front and side façade of Madam Alive Ivers's two-story brothel, which was located in Sturgis, South Dakota. SOUTH DAKOTA STATE HISTORICAL SOCIETY, SOUTH DAKOTA DIGITAL ARCHIVES, 2012-01-23-335

several other soldiers with K Company from Fort Meade stood outside the business throwing rocks and cursing at the occupants inside. Moments before the rowdy, intoxicated group had begun pelting the two-story bordello with stones, one of the men had cut the electrical wires leading to the house, casting it into darkness. Owing to their unruly behavior, it was 10:30 at night when Koetzle, Private Joseph C. Miner, and more than fifteen other infantrymen had been evicted from the business by the feisty madam who ran the resort. Less than two weeks prior, the men had been thrown from the premises for the same reason.

In retaliation, the soldiers had gathered every rock and pebble in sight that July evening and had begun destroying the property. The misguided troops were assaulting the house with another volley of rubble when shots from a Winchester automatic rang out. Koetzle, Miner, and the other men scattered to avoid the spray of bullets.[20]

When the magazine of the gun was empty, all but two of the soldiers emerged unscathed. Private Koetzle had been shot through the head and Private Miner had been hit in the chest. Both men were transported to the post hospital. Koetzle died shortly after arriving, while Miner was in critical condition and, in time, made a full recovery. Poker Alice was arrested and charged with the shooting death of Private Koetzle. Six prostitutes were also taken into custody. The gun the notorious madam used was found outside the door of her house, and the magazine was found lying on Alice's bed. A box of shells was found under the bed.[21]

In addition to being charged with killing a man, Alice was charged with violating the state law prohibiting the operation of a house of ill repute. Her bond was set at $1,000. The bond for the women who worked for her was set at $200 each. The five patrons in the brothel at the time Alice opened fire on the soldiers were taken to jail along with the business owner and her employees. Each man was fined fifteen for frequenting a house of prostitution.[22]

Alice was scheduled to appear in court in September 1913, but a few weeks before the hearing, state and city authorities decided not to prosecute. The facts of the case laid out for the judge showed that the madam had acted justly in defending her property and life, and she was released. Alice and the women who worked for her returned to their jobs soon after.[23]

Poker Alice's gambling house and bordello continued to peacefully service the Fort Meade clientele until 1924. Two separate incidents that year prompted law enforcement to investigate Alice's business. Both incidents involved prohibition violations. On February 20, 1924, Rose Fillbach, one of the soiled doves at Alice's brothel, was arrested on the premises when moonshine was found in her room. The man she'd been seeing claimed the liquor was his and Rose was let out of jail.[24]

Four months later, Alice's resort was raided by the sheriff and his officers on a hunt for alcohol. More than a gallon of moonshine was discovered, and Poker Alice and five men visiting the women in her employ were arrested. She was released after paying a hefty fine for her transgression. The following year, Alice was arrested for operating a house of prostitution. The seventy-four-year-old woman spent a few days in jail and again paid a fine. To justify what she did for a living, Alice insisted that much of the money she made at her business was used to help Black Hills residents in need. "If I had all the money that I have passed out . . . I would be rich," historians noted she remarked, "And there would be many haunting faces looking up at me from the past."[25]

An article in the June 6, 1927, edition of the *Rapid City Journal* announced that Poker Alice was going to take some time off from work to visit her sisters in Virginia for a few weeks. "Poker Alice, who was acquainted with Buffalo Bill, Wild Bill Hickok, Calamity Jane, Deadwood Dick, and many other of the famous individuals of the early days, was in Rapid City Friday," the article read. "She was here to renew old acquaintances and to inspect Rapid City. . . . She has been in the Hills for many years and enjoys nothing better than relating incidents of early Black Hills days." Alice returned from her trip on September 28, 1927.[26]

Prior to leaving town to visit family, Alice had informed friends and newspaper editors that, along with former *Kansas City Star* and *Denver Post* reporter Courtney Ryley Cooper, she was writing an "interesting sketch on her experiences in Arizona, Colorado, Wyoming, and the Black Hills." Alice's story entitled "Easy Come, Easy Go," was published in the December 1927 edition of the *Saturday Evening Post*. "Easy Come, Easy

Go" was about Poker Alice's life as a woman gambler in various mining towns.[27]

> *I had set my poker face and chewed my big black cigars and brought the cards from the faro box in practically every big camp of the West before this time. I simply cite the journey as an instance of what the gambler of the old days—man or woman—would undergo to reach a new camp and to be on the ground floor when the boom really broke.[28]*
>
> *The term "professional gambler" has a greatly different meaning today from what it possessed forty or more years ago. Then, it was not an outlaw practice to live by one's wits and one's ability to outguess the other person in a contest of cards. Dishonesty and crookedness were not the constant companions of games of chance. The gambler played because he loved it for the thrill of the turn of a card or a tight pinch in a contest with persons as sharp as he. Dishonesty hurt the thrill; when crookedness came to gambling, the real professionals quit, leaving the game to be taken by men – and women – who should have been called professional crooks instead.[29]*
>
> *I dealt faro in old Fort Fetterman when the soldiers were there— a fort, incidentally, that has been abandoned now for more than thirty years. I saw Bob Ford killed just as I came off the afternoon faro shift in his gambling hall at Creede. I've won and lost in Alamosa, in Del Norte, in El Paso, in San Marcial; during the boom days of Leadville, Georgetown, Central City, and when miners' money was plentiful in Lead and Deadwood and a score of other camps; but in all that time I handled a cold deck only once and that for a joke.[30]*

Alice elaborated on her card playing skills in the story and told of other women gamblers who helped pave the way for her, women such as Madam Mustache, Haltershanks Eva, and China Mary. She also described gambling life in locations such as Creede, Colorado; Cheyenne, Wyoming; and El Paso, Texas.[31]

> *In the Cactus gambling hall in El Paso I once saw a famous financier of the West lose $34,000 on what we called in those days shoot-mouth.*

In other words, he had brought but little money with him when he entered the place, and, losing that, had begun to borrow from the game to make his bets. When he retired from the gambling hall, there was no promises, no agreements, no signing of notes or writing of checks. It was an affair of honor; everybody knew that the next morning the colonel would arrive and, in courtly fashion, hand over to the game keeper $34,000 in bank notes in payment of his honest debts. That was in fair-and-square days.[32]

Against that, I have seen men with their fingers sandpapered until the blood oozed through the skin. Card marking at that time was done by very fine indentations made with a pin or needle. The crook, as he dealt, must have fingers sensitive enough to read markings that would pass unnoticed in the ordinary man's hands; and the person who helped these men the most was the crooked saloon keeper.[33]

Other [mining] camps beckoned me, among them Deadwood and Lead, in the heart of the last frontier of America's various mining rushes in the Black Hills. . . . There was a well-known character there who would take a stranger into a back room and with a deck of cards show the stranger almost inconceivable feats of manipulation, hereby promoting a partnership by which he announced that he could win all the money in the world.[34]

But when he got into a game with the sharp eyes of professional gamblers upon him, the courage necessary to that crooked skill wilted and he became only a frightened, exceedingly bad player who lost his stacks of chips almost as soon as they were set before him.[35]

One night in Deadwood, I felt the urge of luck and the stronger urge of gambling. I bucked the game with disastrous results to my own money. Then I took my husband's money and gambled that, too. The result was the same. Broke, flat broke, I looked about for a new stake and thought of Mike Russell, a pioneer saloon keeper in Deadwood.[36]

Women were not allowed in Russell's place of business; only one was ever to break the rule—Calamity Jane—and that only because she dressed like a man and acted so like a man that the rule against femininity hardly held for her.[37]

It is still good to play, still a thrill to look at the faces about a [poker] table and to know that you are matching your brains against those of whom card playing is a passion. But I want those men, in these new and hectic days, to be ones with years of friendship behind them. Otherwise, I obey the signs of the Pullman cars: Don't Play Cards with Strangers.[38]

In late 1928, Poker Alice run afoul of the law again and was arrested for "keeping a house of ill repute" and "possession of intoxicating liquor." She was found guilty and sentenced to a six month stay in the state prison at Sioux Falls.[39]

Friends of the elderly madam appealed to South Dakota governor William J. Bulow for mercy. Alice was in poor health, and they didn't think she would survive incarceration. Several people in Deadwood and surrounding areas signed a petition asking the governor to grant Alice a full pardon. He did so on December 19, 1928.[40]

"Poker Alice, or Alice Tubbs, is behaving fairly good following her receipt of a pardon from Gov. W. J. Bulow yesterday which released her from a jail sentence in connection with the conviction of a charge of running a house of ill repute, it was learned from Meade County officials this afternoon," the December 21, 1928, edition of the *Rapid City Journal* read. "When asked today how Poker Alice was behaving, Sheriff Barnes of Sturgis said she was 'doing pretty well,' but added, 'there was room for improvement.'"[41]

Seven months after Alice was released from prison, a Catholic priest stopped by to visit her at her home and discovered that she was seriously ill. Her doctor called on her but couldn't determine the problem. She refused to go to the hospital for testing and decided to stay in bed until the ailment passed. For a time, her health was improving. Alice became well enough to travel to Chicago to watch the baseball games between the Philadelphia Athletics and the Chicago Cubs. The seventy-eight-year-old woman's trip to see the World Series was reported in several South Dakota newspapers.[42]

"The announced intention of Poker Alice to wager a few dollars on the Chicago Cubs while she is East watching the World Series caused no surprise to Black Hills citizens, and, indeed, recalls some other bets that the lady in the case has made," the October 8, 1929, edition of the *Argus Leader* read.

> *One in particular is well remembered by old time ball fans in this little village. It was along about 1912 when Deadwood and Lead were in a baseball frenzy. Open gambling was the vogue, and thousands of dollars changed hands during the year. Unable to agree on either town as the place for playing the final big money game of the season, they came here and played on a baseball diamond hurriedly manufactured out of a corn field.*[43]
>
> *Both teams were spiked to the limit with outside talent. Deadwood's pitcher was Miller Steele, former University of South Dakota player, now with the South Dakota state securities commission. Lead used Primley, who had been pitching some good ball in the sandhills of Nebraska. It was a warm game, but finally Lead forged ahead. Leading 5 to 2, the Lead City partisans got on Poker Alice's nerves. She had bet her wad on Deadwood, the scene of the majority of her professional gambling exploits, and a Lead sport's fan sought to tantalize her by offering further bets.*[44]
>
> *Finally, one of them offered to "bet my watch against $5." He had borrowed an Ingersoll from a boy in the crowd, but Poker Alice, game to the core, refused to back down when he pulled the cheap timepiece, and went through with the bet.*[45]
>
> *The finale must have been interesting to the old lady by reason of the fact that in the eighth inning George Toothacre, who had been with Brush, Colorado, when that little town won the* Denver Post *tournament a few days before, crashed out a homer for Deadwood with the bases loaded, to the financial advantage of Poker Alice to the tune of several hundred dollars and a cheap watch. Poker Alice, according to her own statement, got more "kick out of the tick" of that watch than she did out of her money winnings.*[46]

Poker Alice was often invited to take part in parades and other festivities celebrating the history of the Black Hills. She would sit on the back of an elaborately decorated float, dressed in a dark suit, a man's gray shirt, and regulation army cavalry hat, and wave to the throngs of people who cheered for her as she passed by. City founders and area residents recognized her contribution to Deadwood's colorful past praising her business sense and her genius at the poker table. Not everyone agreed that a gambler and madam should be publicly honored. Many people believed the "wonderful women who pioneered the western country and who had been responsible for its goodness" should be commemorated instead.[47]

In February 1930, Alice was hospitalized in Rapid City and was rushed to surgery to have gallstones removed. Doctors were hopeful she'd make a full recovery and be able to return home. Sadly, that was not the case. Alice Ivers died on February 27 at the age of seventy-nine. She was laid to rest at the Catholic cemetery in Sturgis. Her estate, which at one time estimated to be worth millions, had been reduced to fifty dollars and a few possessions.[48]

6

MADAM BELLE HASKELL AND THE DEMISE OF MAGGIE BROADWATER

FROM THE BEGINNING, THERE WAS A SECTION OF DEADWOOD INTO which respectable citizens would seldom venture, and if they did, it was only under cover of darkness. That area of town was known as the "Bad Lands." Chinese residents were relegated to that section of Deadwood Gulch, as well as most dance halls, saloons, and brothels. The Bad Lands attracted desperate and ruthless men and women convinced their criminal acts would go unpunished; that is at least until law and order could be firmly established in the unmanaged town. Soiled doves were often at the heart of the illegal activities. Some were thieves who stole from other prostitutes who worked with them at various houses of ill repute, some were perpetrators or victims of assault, and others were victims of murder or murderers themselves. The professional women who ran profitable businesses in the Bad Lands were subject to arrest and violence. Only the most brazen attempted to survive and some of them failed in trying.

Belle Haskell had managed her own house, known as the 400, for more than a decade when one of the women in her employ was brutally killed by another prostitute working at the bordello. The well-known madam had opened the bordello in 1880 and, over the years, had been taken into custody for selling alcohol without a license, been beaten by inebriated customers, had her home vandalized and her possessions stolen.[1]

The news that Belle's employee, Austie Trevyr, had murdered Maggie McDermott came as a shock to her and the other women at the house. The murder took place at the popular Badland's tavern the Mascotte

Saloon. Both Austie and Maggie had been keeping company with a gambler named Frank DeBelloy. According to the December 19, 1893, edition of the *Daily Deadwood Pioneer Times*, DeBelloy and Maggie became intimate in the spring of 1891, and for a time their relationship seemed unshakable. The trouble between the two began when DeBelloy took up with another woman. Maggie was slain by the insanely jealous rival, and the crime made headlines throughout the territory.[2]

Three months after Austie Trevyr was arrested for premeditated murder, Belle suffered the loss of yet another of her girls. Nellie Stanley, a twenty-three-year-old woman from Chicago took a job at the 400 in January 1894. Her background was tragic. While still a teenager, her father had intimidated her into marrying a man that was physically abusive. Nellie traveled east to get away from her cruel husband. After a few weeks, she decided to return in hope that the thought of losing her had made him rethink his actions and change his ways. Time apart only made the man bitter and vicious. He refused to take Nellie back. Alone, with no prospects or money, she came west and took a job at a house of ill fame.[3]

Nellie was a quiet, polite, and sad woman who kept to herself. On March 19, 1894, she informed Belle and her coworkers she wasn't feeling well. She complained of having a sore throat and pains in her head. She retired to her room and took a lethal dose of Antikamnia, a drug to help rid sufferers of bad headaches and fever. Nellie was found later in the evening, unconscious. Doctors were called to Belle's home to try and revive her employee, but they were unsuccessful. The women at the brothel who knew Nellie best believed she committed suicide because she was ashamed of the life she felt forced to live.[4]

For the most part, Belle ran an orderly house with few problems. Patrons came and went on a regular basis, never failing to pay for services rendered. Belle wasn't always as quick to pay debts owed. In November 1895, local physician W. W. Torrence took the madam to court because she owed him for the regular examinations he gave her girls. The outstanding bill was $30.50. Legal action had to be taken to retrieve funds she owed at clothing and grocery stores in town too. Belle had a habit of charging items to her account at various businesses and taking months to pay.[5]

Stagecoaches carrying soiled doves arrived in Deadwood routinely. Some of the women worked for Madam Belle Haskell. COURTESY OF DEADWOOD HISTORY, INC. ADAMS MUSEUM COLLECTION, DEADWOOD, SD

It wasn't as though she didn't have money. The 400 was one of the most profitable bordellos in Deadwood. In the spring of 1892, Belle parlayed some of the sizeable income she had amassed to move to a larger house. After remodeling a mansion on Wall Street to fit her needs, she had each room furnished with new beds, sofas, and crystal fixtures. She then had fancy invitations made and sent to two hundred prominent men in the area requesting their attendance at an open house. The editorial staff at the *Black Hills Daily Times* speculated the event would be well attended.[6]

Belle never promoted her business to be anything other than a brothel. She never promised the women who came to work for her a platform to sing or dance. She was welcoming to all who wanted a job at the 400 and offered them a safe, clean environment to entertain guests. Belle wasn't particularly inquisitive and wasn't always aware of the ages of the women working for her. It wasn't until Lawrence County deputy sheriff James Harris paid Belle a visit in February 1898 to ask about one of the courtesans at the house that she learned a fifteen-year-old girl was in her employ. The young woman's father had written a letter to law enforcement agents in Deadwood stating he believed his daughter was in the Black Hills and leading a life of shame and requested that she be found.[7]

Deputy Sheriff Harris's search led to Belle Haskell's place. When the girl was located, she agreed to leave Belle's and stay at a more wholesome home until her father was informed and could get her. According to the February 9, 1898, edition of the *Deadwood Evening Independent*, the teenage girl had left home to live with her sister in Sundance after some "unpleasantries" with her father. From there she went to Spearfish, where she was supposed to stay until her brother came to take her home. She left before he arrived and made her way to Belle Fourche. She then traveled to Deadwood where she had been for three weeks prior to the authorities catching up to her.[8]

The young woman told Deputy Harris she would go home if her father sent her money, because she had no money of her own to pay for her travels. She told him her parents were poor and lived on a ranch in Montana. She didn't believe they could raise any money to send her. Deputy Harris explained to her that he wasn't sure how to proceed in case her father didn't send money, as the laws in South Dakota made no provisions for such cases from outside the territory.[9]

The Salvation Army offered to provide the funds needed to pay the young woman's transportation to a refuge in Omaha, Nebraska. The teenager's father agreed that's where his daughter should be sent because he feared she would run away again if returned to Montana. Even though the woman had been working for Belle, she did not feel compelled to contribute to helping her leave the area. The absence of the young woman meant a decrease in the money coming into the bordello.

Belle's focus was on running a profitable business, and little else interested her. Between 1898 and 1906, Madam Haskell increased the number of women at her house and reaped the financial reward. Nothing out of the ordinary occurred personally or professionally in Belle's world until the winter of 1907, when she was once again tangentially involved in a murder.[10]

In late November, Belle was visiting her friend and fellow business owner Benny Fowler at her room at the Mansion Hotel and Bar. The two had plans to go to dinner and attend a party afterward. Benny had traveled to Deadwood from Belle Fourche where she operated another brothel. The reason for the trip was twofold. Benny wanted to see Belle and she wanted to get away from a man who had been bothering her.[11]

Prentice Bernard, alias Vinegar Rowan, a cowpuncher and sheepherder from Montana, had spent time with Benny in Belle Fourche and become infatuated with her. He challenged customers who visited her, threatening to beat the men if they didn't stay away. She hoped when he passed through Belle Fourche again and learned she wasn't there he would ride on and forget her. That wasn't the case, however. When Vinegar learned where Benny had gone, he followed her. He had been in trouble with the law in Deadwood a few times before because he wouldn't leave her alone. He was crazy with jealousy over the men she met and, on December 7, 1907, pulled a knife on a bartender whom he overheard talking about Benny and assaulted a cook named Dick Moran for the same thing.[12]

Frustrated with Vinegar's actions and his relentless pursuit, Benny hurried back to Belle Fourche. Again, she hoped her clear rejection would persuade him to drop his fixation and move on with his life. After a day with no sign of Vinegar, Benny thought the coast was clear and returned to Deadwood to continue her visit with Belle. She had no way of knowing that Vinegar had never left Deadwood. He was so distressed over the way Benny had treated him he decided to get drunk and stay drunk. The manager of the Mansion Hotel and Bar where Vinegar was doing most of his drinking demanded the rancher give him his gun while he was there. Vinegar did so but asked several times for the weapon to be returned.

His request was denied because he was considered too drunk to handle a weapon.[13]

On December 9, a sober Vinegar appeared at the bar shortly after 5:30 in the evening and asked again for his gun. He told the bartender he was going to take the train back to Belle Fourche and needed all his possessions before leaving. His gun was returned to him.[14]

Benny was upstairs in her hotel room dressing to go out with Belle, blissfully unaware Vinegar was anywhere around. At 5:45 p.m., she called out to Dick Moran, who was in the room next to hers, and asked him to fasten the hooks on the back of her dress. He hurried to Benny and was standing behind her, in front of a bureau, buttoning her dress when Vinegar appeared in the door with his gun in hand.[15]

Without any warning he began shooting, the first bullet striking Dick Moran in the back. Moran fell, and he [Vinegar] turned the gun on Benny, firing two shots but missing her. She dropped to the floor and crawled under the bed but almost immediately came out at the foot and as she arose to her feet, Vinegar fired another shot which missed her and struck the wall a few inches over her left shoulder. She then grappled with him, turned him around, and forced him to the door.[16]

Just as he crossed the threshold, the fifth shot was fired, which struck him on the right side of the upper lip and passed through his head, coming out on the left side above the ear. It was this last act that was witnessed by Belle Haskell who had just come from an adjoining room, on hearing the other shots. Vinegar fell forward across the narrow hall and dropped on his face, dead.[17]

One of the bartenders was the first to reach the scene after the shooting, and it was a gruesome sight that met his gaze. Vinegar was lying in a deep pool of blood, his teeth scattered about the floor, and his brains oozing out from a ghastly hole in his head. Moran was lying on the floor of the room, supporting his head on his hand. As the bartender entered, Dick said, "I guess I'm done for, Bill," and asked for a cigarette which he smoked with apparent relish.[18]

There was a scene of disorder and riot throughout the house among the women who occupied rooms on the floor, but it was quickly quelled when the sheriff and police arrived. Dr. Howe, the coroner, was called and, after a hasty examination of Moran had him removed to St. Joseph hospital.[19]

It is the opinion of those who have studied the features of the case, that Vinegar did not intend to shoot himself with the bullet which caused his death. It was evidently his intention to kill the woman, as he had already fired three shots at her, and it is not probable that he would have disposed of his own case, even though he might have contemplated ultimate suicide, until he had finished her. She was forcing him out of the room, walking behind and gripping him by the shoulders. He doubtless attempted to reach over his left shoulder and fire another shot at her, but in the uncertainty of the aim in that position discharged the bullet into this own face.[20]

Belle Haskell used the notoriety she gained from the various newspaper articles in which she was featured to her advantage. Curious patrons sought her and her house out to do business.

Rumored fallen angels such as Maggie Broadwater tried desperately to avoid the limelight during her short career. The twenty-one-year-old woman's occupation was only made public when she jumped from the window on the third floor of the Fairmont Hotel where she worked. Born in Callaway, Missouri, Margaret, or Maggie as she was better known, ventured west, and settled in Colorado where she found work at a house of ill repute. Eventually, she relocated to Thermopolis, Wyoming, where she met a gentleman customer and fell in love. The couple parted ways and Maggie traveled to Deadwood. Her profession remained the same, but she used the name Margaret Gillet while on the job.[21]

Maggie attempted to drown her sorrows in alcohol over the love she lost, but it only made her feel worse. Consumed with remorse, she decided to take her own life. Maggie's fall was cushioned by a patch of soft mud under her window, but she did sustain several injuries, including a compound fracture of the wrist, broken ribs, and a broken jaw. She was transported to St. Joseph Hospital where at first it seemed she would recover. The following day doctors determined she was suffering with serious internal injuries. One of her kidneys was ruptured and her

Maggie Broadwater jumped from the third floor of the Fairmont Hotel in 1907. SOUTH DAKOTA STATE HISTORICAL SOCIETY, SOUTH DAKOTA DIGITAL ARCHIVES, 2008-05-23-022

liver was severely damaged. The August 31, 1907, edition of the *Daily Pioneer Times* reported that Maggie "suffered intense agony at times but remained conscious until within forty minutes of the time of her death."[22]

Maggie's relatives in Colorado were notified of her demise but never came to claim her body. She was laid to rest at Mount Moriah Cemetery.

1

Madam May Brown and the Tragic Life and Death of Maud Lee

Ottoman and Johanne Gotsch never knew what led their daughter Anna to a life of prostitution in the Black Hills. Born on December 2, 1859, in Saxony, Germany, she was a precocious child who enjoyed spending time with her five brothers and four sisters and possessed a talent for painting. The Gotsch family moved to America when Anna was four years old, and they settled in Iowa. For a time, Anna considered becoming a teacher, then she met a soldier from Illinois named Edward Piergue and decided to be a wife. The couple traveled from post to post between 1873 and 1879. Their son, Lawrence, was born in October 1879 in St. Joseph, Missouri, and their daughter, Josephine, in 1882 in Humboldt, Iowa.[1]

Not long after the birth of their second child, Edward decided to abandon his military career and take up prospecting. Gold had been discovered in Idaho, and Edward believed he could find a fortune. He left Anna and their children behind at her parents' home. Within weeks of Edward leaving, Anna set off on her own. By the spring of 1884, she was working at a house of ill repute in Deadwood.[2]

Anna Piergue changed her name to May Brown, and in time, she earned enough working for various madams in town that she went into business for herself. May's house was small but a favorite of many men in the area. It wasn't long until she opened a brothel in Rapid City. The local newspapers reported the numerous departures and arrivals via stage May

93

took traveling back and forth between businesses. She often made the journey with fellow courtesans Lottie Bright and May Melville.[3]

Lottie, Mattie Smith, May Melville, Flora Hogan, and May Brown were all members of the same profession and good friends as well. They had a reputation for hosting wild parties where alcohol was in abundance. After an all-night celebration in early May 1886, the women decided to literally paint the town red. They paraded up and down the streets with paint brushes and buckets of red paint and marked various buildings with the scarlet color. When May thought the behavior of the group she was with had gotten too far out of control, she attempted to put a stop to the frivolity by leveling her pistol at them and firing a couple of shots. The police responded to the gunfire and arrested the four. May paid a ten dollar fine for discharging her weapon in public. The others had to pay a similar amount for drunk and disorderly conduct.[4]

Encounters with the law did not intimidate May Brown. Like many career sporting women of the time, dealing with the police and the courts was part of the job. She wasn't surprised when she was taken into custody seven months after the pistol incident. It was Christmas, and a steady stream of customers had stopped by her house in Rapid City to spend time with the ladies who worked there. Authorities were called to May's place to address a complaint made against the business. May was taken into custody along with two of the women who worked for her and one male patron. Madam Brown was fined ten dollars for keeping a house of ill fame. May Howard, May Melville, and Frank Hamilton were each fined five dollars. An article in the December 21, 1886, edition of the *Rapid City Journal* noted that additional warrants had been issued for the arrest of others who were employed at the bordello and those that frequented the business. "This move of the police is in the right direction, and it is to be hoped the officers will have the moral courage to keep it up," the article read. "These women have flaunted their shame in the face of decency for so long unmolested that their effrontery has become almost intolerable. A few applications of the ordinances will have the effect of ridding the city of at least a part of the pest."[5]

May encountered several men who wanted more from her than a single evening. She spurned the affections of all but one. Early upon her arrival in the Black Hills, May Melville introduced May to a renegade named John Tilford. He had been involved in a series of petty crimes from St. Louis to Cheyenne. Tilford traveled to Deadwood to escape a breach of promise suit filed by a woman in Kentucky he left at the altar. He met May shortly after he arrived. The two were often seen together and he visited her at her brothel in town and in Rapid City. John spent time at other bordellos too, and he was seldom civil during his visits. He was violent. Prostitutes Georgia King and May Melville were victims of his attacks. In September 1886, both King and Melville had John charged with assault and battery. When the matter was finally brought before a judge, Tilford was given the option to pay a five-dollar fine or spend two days in jail. He paid the fine.[6]

John Tilford and his friend John Hamilton opened the Headquarters Saloon on Lee Street on December 1, 1887. They offered fine liquor and cigars, and May made sure the establishment always had soiled doves present. She helped furnish Tilford's saloon with customers, and he drove business her way in exchange. The steady increase in traffic at May's led to the hiring of more girls. The brothel's further gain in popularity did not go unnoticed by authorities.[7]

In mid-January, May was indicted for keeping a bawdy house. She paid yet another fine and returned to work. The longer May's relationship with John went on, the more trouble the madam found herself. Authorities continually charged her for operating bordellos, and she was implicated in the theft of alcohol from warehouses in Sturgis. John Tilford and his cohort, Robert Lawrence, were arrested for the crime on August 21, 1888. The case was eventually dismissed when a key witness came up missing.[8]

When Tilford was arrested two months later for conspiring to rob the pay train on the Black Hills and Fort Pierre railroad, May was in court again. Police believed she might have offered her help in planning the deed. Tilford and five others planned to first wreck the train and then rob the paymaster of the more than $12,000 reported to be on board. The planning of the crime allegedly took place at Tilford's saloon. Law enforcement was alerted to the robbery and were able to stop Tilford and the others before the job was done. Members of the gang Tilford was with confessed to authorities the horses to be used in the botched holdup belonged to him. It was rumored that May aided Tilford in acquiring the animals and had fresh mounts in the waiting for the getaway.[9]

Both May and Tilford denied involvement in the planned attempted train robbery. The article in the October 14, 1888, edition of the *Rapid City Journal* questioned their credibility given their prior run-ins with the law and noted that "it would seem, on the whole, that it might be amiss to give Telford [*sic*] and his female consort an opportunity to tell what they know of the whole affair, or if they know anything about it. It is a reasonable presumption, from all the surrounding circumstances, that they are not entirely in the dark."[10]

After a full investigation, Tilford was charged with larceny and his trial set for December 1888. May was in the courtroom every day during the hearing. Witnesses testified that after the criminals escaped the attempted holdup, they met at May's brothel. The evidence against Tilford proved to be overwhelming. He was found guilty and sentenced to fifteen years hard labor at the territorial penitentiary in Sioux Falls. May and Tilford corresponded until his early release in 1894, and he returned to Deadwood.[11]

May kept busy during Tilford's absence. Her association with the convicted felon and allegations that she had a part in the attempted train robbery did not adversely affect business. The brothels in both Deadwood and Rapid City continued to do well. May managed to keep her name out of the papers until the summer of 1891 when she had a prostitute named Blanche Doe arrested for theft. Blanche stole a dress valued at five dollars that belonged to May. The judge hearing the case was able to settle the matter quickly by ordering the defendant to return the garment and apologize.[12]

May Brown, formally known as Anna Piergue, divorced her husband Edward on February 3, 1892. She had begun divorce proceedings four years prior before Tilford's legal troubles became known. She had been too overwhelmed with that situation to file the paperwork and see it through at that time. The February 4, 1892, edition of the *Black Hills Daily Times* announced the decree for divorce had been granted and reminded readers May was "a member of the demimonde."[13]

Authorities marched May Brown and two of her employees, May Hamilton and Mollie Smith, before a judge in Rapid City on the charge of keeping houses of ill fame. The three were summoned to court after a nineteen-year-old boy was arrested for frequenting May's brothels in Deadwood and Rapid City. The young man pled guilty and was fined five dollars, but his father insisted the madam, and the other two women, answer for their parts in the illegal activity.[14]

The police had warned Madam Brown in the past that she was not allowed to do business with boys, but she had ignored the order and now must suffer the consequences. She was fined five dollars and had to pay the court costs. When she left the courthouse, the chief of police vowed to make life "a trifle burdensome for this class of our population." When the wife of P. H. O'Leary learned he'd been spending evenings with May in the summer of 1893, she pressed charges against him for adultery. Friends of both O'Leary and May got word to the unfaithful husband that his arrest was eminent, and he fled to North Dakota. Law enforcement was still on his trail when Tilford arrived back in Deadwood in late August 1893.[15]

May and Tilford took up where they'd left off and they were rarely seen without the other. It wasn't long before the two were once again in trouble with the law. The violent incident involving the pair happened at May's Deadwood bordello. "Shortly after midnight on Monday night, a shooting scrape occurred in this city in a house conducted by May Brown," the May 2, 1894, edition of the *Argus Leader* reported.[16]

After knocking beer glasses around promiscuously they proceeded to clean out the establishment, and during the melee which ensued, John Tilford appeared on the scene, fired two shots, one of which took effect in the ankle of Michael Mahoney, one of the participants. Mahoney was taken to the Exchange Hotel, where he had the wound dressed yesterday afternoon.[17]

No arrests were made until yesterday when Sheriff Zollars arrested John Tilford and May Brown on the charge of shooting with intent to kill. The parties were taken before Judge Worth when Tilford entered the plea of not guilty and waved an examination. He was bound over to appear before the grand jury in the sum of one hundred dollars, which was furnished. The case against May Brown was continued for several days.[18]

May was eventually acquitted of the charges. Tilford failed to show up for his court date, and his bond was forfeited. May and Tilford's relationship appeared to have ended after the shooting. He left South Dakota and wasn't heard from again until he shot another man during a card game at Fort Steele, fifteen miles east of Rawlins, Wyoming.[19]

Lightning struck May's Rapid City brothel in late July 1895. The fire that started as a result was quickly extinguished, and all the inhabitants escaped without injury. One of the boarders in the front room of the house was struck by the bolt of lightning, and for a time May feared the woman would die. The bolt struck her on the left shoulder, passed over the body to the right side, down the right leg, and tore the shoe from her foot. May was in the rear of the house at the time of the strike and was knocked out of her chair.[20]

Soiled doves enjoying a drink at a brothel in 1902. AUTHOR'S COLLECTION

Life passed without incident for May over the next nine years. She was hospitalized at St. Joseph Hospital in April 1905 because she suffered with a disease called edema. May died on October 29, 1905. Her children traveled to Deadwood to retrieve her body. Her remains were sent to Dakota City, Iowa, where she was laid to rest.[21]

Soiled dove Maud Lee worked at a house in Deadwood not far from May Brown's business. Where she came from and what her real name might have been is lost in history. What is known is that she was a sporting girl who was employed at brothels in Pierre, Lead, Sturgis, and Rapid City. She arrived in Deadwood on December 1, 1885, and four days later was the victim of a beating at the hand of another prostitute. The assailant was arrested for assault and battery and fined twelve dollars for her violent behavior.[22]

Maud began the year of 1886 troubled with a medical issue. By the time she traveled to Rapid City to see a doctor, she was "dangerously ill." She returned to Deadwood in April feeling better than she had in several weeks. She went back to work, alternating between the various houses in which she was employed.[23]

A civil action was brought against Maud in June 1889 for nonpayment of thirty-five dollars. She claimed to have no money and couldn't pay, but the complainant accused her of "fraudulent insolvency." The businessowner to whom Maud owed a debt claimed she did have money but gave it to a friend to keep for her until the situation was resolved. After hearing the facts, the judge ruled in favor of Maud and dismissed the case.[24]

In 1891, Maud was arrested for prostitution, along with three of her other coworkers in Pierre. They were ordered to vacate the brothel and leave the city. Maud moved her things to the bordello in Deadwood, but her career as a courtesan in Pierre did not end. On April 4, 1894, she had one of her customers, a man named Dick Williams, arrested for shooting up her room with a pistol.[25]

It came as a shock to the soiled doves in Deadwood and surrounding areas when Maud Lee died on September 25, 1895. The peculiar circumstances surrounding her death led authorities to launch an investigation.

A coroner was summoned, and a jury was impaneled. A prominent female physician was suspected of performing an illegal procedure on Maud. At an inquest, the coroner's jury agreed the courtesan died as a result of an abortion Dr. Alice S. Baird gave the deceased. The doctor was subsequently arrested for manslaughter. She was found guilty, paid a fine, and moved out of the Black Hills. Dr. Baird died in Mitchell, South Dakota, in November 1900.[26]

8

The Trials of Thelma Campbell

Minnie Henderson, a prostitute working at Madam Annie Woods's brothel in Lead, South Dakota, crawled to a corner of her room, sobbing loudly and writhing in pain. Her face was a fountain of blood. The sporting girls who worked across the hall from her were on either side of the distressed woman trying to help. They covered the deep cuts across Minnie's cheeks, nose, and forehead with thick towels and bed-sheets. Curious inmates in the house raced to the room to find out the reason for the commotion. Some stood frozen, their eyes wide with terror; others hurried off to find the police and a doctor. Minnie wept and cried; her hands cupped over her bleeding ears.[1]

Thelma Campbell, a frantic courtesan with unruly hair and desperately pale skin, ran as fast as she could down the dusty road out of Lead on her way to Deadwood. She was wearing a kimono that barely covered her undergarments and carrying a cloth bag, bulging with whatever she could stuff in it at a moment's notice. Carving up Minnie's face had been unexpected. After the deed was done, Thelma wanted to get away as quickly as possible. She'd had no time to dress or pack properly. She planned to hop on a stage leaving Deadwood and make her way to Pierre where she would board a train heading out of South Dakota.[2]

Thelma was apprehended before she made it to the stage, but the arrest didn't come easy. She fought the sheriff's deputies and cursed them all the way to jail. The date she was placed into custody was September 3, 1908.[3]

The *Daily Deadwood Pioneer Times* gave a full report of the attack the day after it occurred:

> *As a result of a jealous quarrel . . . one woman is in the hospital suffering injuries which may prove fatal, and another is in jail in this city. Thelma Campbell and Minnie Henderson came from Kansas City together a few months ago and have, since going to Lead, been at dance halls there. They roomed together, and this caused the altercation with serious results. Each girl wanted the other to give her possession of the room, and, after a quarrel, Thelma seized a razor and proceeded to carve some fancy designs on the anatomy of her roommate.[4]*
>
> *One slash started on the forehead, passing over the cheek and to the neck, missing the jugular vein by a fraction. This wound will disfigure the girl for life. Another thrust extended from under the left arm around the abdomen, requiring fifty stiches to close. Her clothing offered slight protection, and the wound is deep and dangerous.[5]*

Minnie survived the ordeal and, although she was left permanently scarred by the attack, refused to pursue charges against her assailant. The state was bound to take action against Thelma, however, and the judge overseeing the case scheduled the woman's hearing for September 9, 1908. Thelma's bond was set at $500. Minnie's recovery was slow; she had stitches on her face, chest, and neck, which prompted the court to postpone the matter several times. The prosecution wanted Minnie to be well enough to appear at the trial.[6]

Both the victim and accused met in the courtroom on October 2, 1908. The proceedings didn't last long. Minnie explained to the judge that she'd forgiven Thelma and wanted to move on. That act of mercy kept Thelma from being sent to the penitentiary. The sentence she received was thirty days in the county jail, and it was time she had already served.[7]

Minnie and Thelma were back at work at the bawdy house shortly after the case was closed. Less than two weeks later, the pair found themselves in another life-threatening situation when the brothel caught fire. The blaze started on the second floor of the house on Friday, October

Fires like the one Thelma Campbell survived were commonplace in Deadwood. This photo of Deadwood shows the destruction from a fire that began at the Empire Bakery in 1879. COURTESY OF DEADWOOD HISTORY, INC. ADAMS MUSEUM COLLECTION, DEADWOOD, SD

14, 1908, by a lit cigarette placed too close to the curtains. Minnie and Thelma escaped without injury, but two courtesans died in the fire, and six others suffered burns or broken bones trying to get out of the building. A customer named Frank Askine also lost his life in the fire.[8]

The brothel was rebuilt by the end of the year, and Thelma and Minnie returned to the job. Minnie eventually tired of the business and decided to leave the area. She was with several other passengers onboard a streetcar in Des Moines, Iowa, when the vehicle was struck by a passenger train. She was seriously hurt in the accident.[9]

Thelma's career as a courtesan in the Black Hills thrived. The publicity surrounding the incident that occurred with Minnie and her subsequent arrest and trial had made her somewhat of a novelty. Curious men sought her out, and one of them captured her heart. When it became clear he did not want a future with Thelma, she became enraged and threatened the woman she believed was the reason for the trouble in their relationship.[10]

On November 22, 1911, Thelma made her way to a local restaurant for dinner. She'd been drinking heavily just before that and, when she arrived at the eatery, decided to kill herself rather than order a meal. She found a butcher knife at the restaurant and started cutting herself. She sliced open her arms in several places before customers intervened and the police were called. She was arrested and bailed out by her employer.[11]

Thelma was in deep despair when she was escorted back to her room at the brothel. Determined to end her life, she took a dose of carbolic acid. It wasn't enough to get the job done, and after a doctor was called to exam her, the police took her into custody for attempted suicide. She pled not guilty at her hearing in February 1912. The court fined her twenty-five dollars and warned her to stay out of trouble. She didn't listen.[12]

On Saturday, April 6, 1912, a fight broke out in one of the saloons in Deadwood between Thelma and another prostitute in town. During the altercation, Thelma smashed a beer bottle over the woman's head, knocking her out and cutting a gash in her scalp. Thelma was immediately arrested and spent the night in jail. The following morning she was released after a $100 bond was paid. At the trial that followed, Thelma was sentenced to eighty days hard labor at a penitentiary in Illinois and, as a condition of parole she might receive, the judge strongly suggested she never return to the Black Hills. It was another directive she chose to ignore. By the fall of 1912 she was back in Deadwood and causing trouble.[13]

Working as a prostitute and flitting in and out of jail, news that a law had been passed prohibiting the transportation of a person with the intent to engage them in prostitution must have missed Thelma. She learned about the Mann Act on October 29, 1912, when she was arrested in Lead. A special agent with the United States Department of Justice charged Thelma with white slavery after discovering she brought five women into the Black Hills from Missouri for the purposes of working in the prostitution trade.[14]

"The charge is a most serious one," the October 30, 1912, edition of the *Lead Daily Call* reported, "and should the Campbell women be found guilty she will be sentenced to one of the federal prisons for a long term of years. The girls in question were brought from Kansas City and entered and became inmates of one of the gilded palaces of sin in Deadwood.[15]

> In order that they would be available as witnesses in the hearing before the commissioner this morning, the women in question were taken into custody last evening. This is the first time that the charge of white slavery has been brought against anyone in the Black Hills, and it is the intention of the federal authorities to push the matter to the limit.[16]
>
> At a hearing before Commissioner Moore, the evidence was so conclusive that the defendant, Thelma Campbell, was held to appear for trial before the next term of the federal court and her bail placed at the sum of $5,000. Unable to give the bond required, the Campbell woman was delivered into the custody of the United States marshal.[17]
>
> Bessie Meyers and Jessie Graham, two of the victims of the bondage of white slavery, who were important witnesses for the prosecution in the case against the Campbell woman, were placed under $500 bonds each and being unable to furnish them were delivered into the custody of the United States marshal to ensure appearance at the trial.[18]

Thelma was taken back to Missouri to stand trial in Kansas City. Her hearing was scheduled for late spring 1913, and authorities estimated she could be sentenced to more than ten years in a penitentiary if found guilty. In April, she accepted a plea of six months in jail if she turned state's evidence. She did so and implicated her former employer, Anna Woods. Woods fled to Canada before she could be taken into custody.[19]

Thelma Campbell served her time and was never seen in the Black Hills again.

Unknown Deadwood prostitute AUTHOR'S COLLECTION

9

THE MURDER OF MAGGIE MCDERMOTT

MAGGIE MCDERMOTT PEERED INTO THE GRIMY WINDOWS OF THE Mascott Saloon and eyed the faces huddled around the bar. When she didn't see who she was looking for, she removed the note tucked in her pocket, tilted it toward the lit oil lamp hanging outside the door, and studied the message. It read, "Frank and I are at the Mascott. Come on. Austie." Maggie exchanged a knowing glance with her friend Hattie Rice as she wadded the note in her hand. Hattie nodded to her, and the women proceeded inside.[1]

The pair weaved through the rowdy patrons in search of Frank and the author of the invitation. The business was crowded. Men and women on a congested dance floor flitted about to a lively song a piano player was pounding out on an instrument badly in need of tuning. Occasionally, the women were stopped and propositioned by men who recognized them as prostitutes from the Gem Variety Theater. After inviting the potential customers to visit them later, Maggie and Hattie continued with their hunt. They asked a busboy for help, and he directed them to a room in the back of the busy tavern.[2]

A gambler named Frank DeBelloy and his date, Austie Trevyr, a sixteen-year-old soiled dove employed at Madam Belle Haskell's house of ill repute, were waiting on the other side of the door when Maggie and Hattie entered. The couple was seated at a table, drinking whiskey. Frank offered Maggie a smile, and before he opened his mouth to speak, a bartender carrying a tray of glasses and a bottle of wine pushed past the two women. When the bartender left the room Austie set a glass in front of

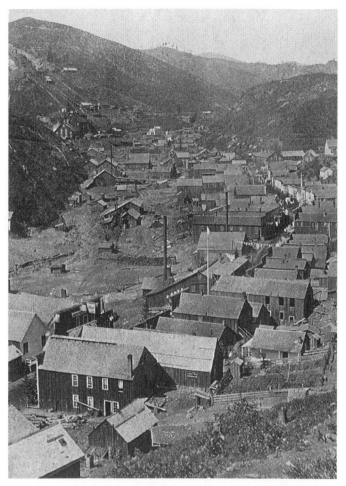

Early days of Deadwood. COURTESY OF LIBRARY OF CONGRESS

Maggie and poured her a drink. "You have your nerve to ask me to drink with you and Frank when I have more claim on him than you," Maggie barked at the teenager, "we having been together for the past three years." Maggie then removed the note Austie wrote that she had wadded up and shoved in her pocket and tore it into pieces.[3]

Austie glared at her rival, cursed at her under her breath, and drank down the last of wine she had poured for Maggie. She then pushed her chair back and stood up, her eyes fixed on Maggie. She reached into the top of her dress and removed a gun. Frightened, Hattie grabbed Maggie's arm and tried to pull her out of the room. Maggie watched as Austie leveled the .32-caliber Smith and Wesson revolver at her and cocked the weapon. "Well, if I can't have him you can't," she spat. The report of the gun was loud. Hattie screamed, and Maggie grabbed her chest and staggered backward. Austie was about to shoot Maggie a second time when Frank grabbed her arm and hand. In the scuffle, the gun went off again.[4]

Maggie sank into a chair, crying, "She shot me." Hattie rushed to her side and tried to help Maggie get to her feet and escort her to an adjoining room. She barely made it across the doorsill when she fell to the floor screaming, "Oh! Hattie! Oh! Hattie! I'm gone." Frank quickly picked the injured woman up and laid her on a sofa. Moments later, Maggie was gone. She died on December 17, 1893.[5]

Austie raced out of the room and asked one of the owners of the saloon to get the police. She was gone by the time the authorities arrived. She ran to Belle Haskell's house to grab her hat and shawl. After letting her employer know she'd shot a woman, she returned to the Mascott and confessed her crime to the investigating officer at the scene. When asked where she got the gun, she bragged that Frank had given it to her as a present. On her way to jail, Austie told the police she had intended shooting Maggie, her friend Hattie, and Frank, and that the second shot she fired was meant for Frank. The arresting officer noted in his report later that day that when he placed Austie in the cell she didn't break down or exhibit any remorse. In his estimation, Austie seemed almost happy she'd killed Maggie McDermott.[6]

Frank was arrested shortly after Austie was placed into custody and subsequently released once his $2,500 bond was paid.[7]

News of the murder spread quickly throughout the Black Hills, and several articles were written about the crime and the parties involved. According to various newspaper articles, Maggie McDermott came west from Sioux City, Iowa, and settled in Deadwood in 1891 after she was hired by Al Swearingen to work at the Gem as an entertainer. Maggie and Frank became romantically involved the same year she arrived in South Dakota. She had been out of town for a few months prior to the shooting.

She returned to Deadwood in late October and she and Frank had seen one another briefly during that time.[8]

Mary Yusta, better known as Austie Trevyr, came to Deadwood from Lincoln, Nebraska, and was the daughter of one of the best known and wealthiest families in the region. The family farm was situated between Crete and Wilbur. She left home in 1892 and began working at a brothel in Lincoln where she went by the names of Birdie Bailey and Babe Lamont. She moved to the Black Hills in August 1893 and took a job at Belle Haskell's house. Frank DeBelloy was one of her regular customers, and their relationship blossomed from there. According to Madam Haskell, Austie was "well-behaved, excepting at times when she would break out into a series of most startling acts." In Belle's opinion, the young woman was mentally unbalanced. "She was a girl who evidently had seen better times, possessed intelligence to a fair degree and was fairly educated, but odd. She possessed a handsome face, figure, and manner."[9]

The December 21, 1893, edition of the *Weekly Pioneer Times* noted that Frank DeBelloy was considered a manly, honest, straightforward man. He minded his own business and had a wide circle of friends. From the evidence adduced at the coroner's jury, he was blameless and had no idea the fatal affair would occur. "His presenting the gun to the girl a day or so before the shooting, while it looks bad shows nothing against him," the *Weekly Pioneer Times* article read. "It does not look reasonable that a man would give a girl a gun and then accompany her in broad daylight to a saloon and decoy an enemy to the room for the express purpose of killing that one.[10]

His presenting the gun to the woman might have occurred this way: She found it in his pocket and took it and he probably let her keep it. His indiscretion was in allowing both girls to think him in love with them. Had he dismissed the deceased, the affair might not have occurred. As she [Maggie] told him a few days before, 'If you love Austie better than you do me, I will return to Sioux City and leave you,' but instead of saying he preferred Austie as he should he told her he cared for her.[11]

According to the coroner's report, the bullet that killed Maggie entered "an inch from the right nipple, penetrated the sixth rib, penetrated the right lobe of the liver and severed the descending aorta or the large main artery from the heart which supplied the entire system with blood, and lodged in the spleen, death was caused by the filling of the lower cavity of the body with blood."[12]

The coroner's jury took the testimony of eight witnesses. Frank DeBelloy refused to give testimony because he said he didn't want to incriminate himself. Among those who did agree to give statements was Officer O. C. Lackous. He explained to the jury that he was the one who arrested Austie and that on the way to jail he asked her if she did the shooting, and she admitted she had. Dr. Howe testified that he assisted another doctor in performing the postmortem examination and confirmed they found an opening in the right breast, apparently made by the bullet. He told the jury that he believed Maggie was in an upright position at the time she was shot, which the course of the bullet indicated. He also noted that Maggie's arm might have been raised.[13]

The verdict of the jury was that Maggie McDermott came to her death by a shot from a pistol in the hands of Austie Trevyr and that the shooting was premeditated.[14]

Several months would pass before Austie would stand trial for murdering Maggie McDermott. During her incarceration in the Deadwood jail, she was allowed visits from friends and Christian ladies' groups who ministered to her spiritual needs. Women from various churches in the area reported to the congregation at large they believed Austie's heart had undergone a change for the better. By the time the case was brought before the circuit court in March 1894, public sympathy was with Austie who was now being referred to by her real name.[15]

Attorney General Hastings of Nebraska, assisted by Captain Murfin and Henry Frawley, were hired to defend the accused. The state was represented by attorney Jonathan Meer who promised to "strain every nerve to secure a conviction."[16]

The trial of Austie Trevyr for the murder of Maggie McDermott began on Thursday, March 1, at nine in the morning. Before the doors of the courtroom were opened, crowds began congregating, awaiting anxiously to rush into the room and secure seats. The jury, made up of twelve men, took its appropriate place at 9:30 a.m., and Judge Jeffrey W. Plowman, who was presiding over the hearing, gave them their instructions. All witnesses were excluded from the courtroom. Nick Saragen, a witness for the prosecution, was the first to take the stand. He testified that he worked at the Mascott Saloon at the time of the killing and that he delivered a note for Maggie from Austie to Hattie Rice.[17]

Michael Donovan testified that he was one of the proprietors of the Mascott and that he found writing paper for Austie, that he saw her write the note and then instructed him to get the note to Maggie. He witnessed Maggie and Hattie come into the saloon and go to the wine room where Frank and Austie were waiting. Shortly afterward, Donovan heard two shots. He dropped the tray of glasses he had in his hand and went into the room where he saw Hattie and Maggie coming out. He testified that Frank and Austie were on the opposite side of the room, scuffling. Donovan shouted for Frank to grab Austie's gun. He heard Maggie announce that she'd been shot and watched her stagger to another room where she collapsed onto the floor. Donovan sent for the doctor. Austie asked him to call the police too.[18]

Hattie Rice then testified. She stated that Maggie had been her roommate and that when Maggie received the note written by Austie the two read it together. The pair then proceeded to the Mascott where they found Frank and Austie. Hattie shared that Austie poured Maggie a drink, which she refused. Maggie said to Austie, "I like your nerve of being here with Frank because you know he is my friend." Heated words were exchanged between Maggie and Austie, but Hattie could not remember everything that was said. She recalled Austie saying, "Well, we will see if you will have him or who will have him." At that, Austie pulled her revolver and announced to Maggie, "You can't have him either." She witnessed two shots fired at Maggie and Maggie dying shortly after being struck by a bullet.[19]

Officer O. C. Lackous took the stand after Hattie and told the jury that when he arrived on the scene, he had seen Maggie lying on a sofa and that her shirt was bloody. He arrested Austie, who readily admitted to the deed.[20]

The state rested its case after hearing testimony from the coroner who described the damage the bullet did to Maggie's vital organs and how the wound killed her.

Soiled dove Dora Deane was the first witness called on behalf of the defense. She was questioned by the defendant's attorneys about a conversation she had had with the deceased in which she threatened Austie. The defense lawyers tried to prove that Maggie communicated those threats to Austie before the shooting. The evidence was rejected by the state's attorney as being irrelevant and immaterial. The court sustained the objection.[21]

Frank DeBelloy then begrudgingly took the stand and testified having known the deceased and defendant. He told the court that he was at the Mascott at the time of the shooting. He testified that he was with Austie at Belle Haskell's 400 brothel before the incident and that he and the accused walked over to the saloon together. They were there ten minutes before Maggie and Hattie came into the room where he and Austie were drinking wine. He shared that Maggie walked extremely fast and looked like she was quite angry. She spoke first, and some words ensued between them, then Maggie started calling Austie vile names. According to Frank, he invited Maggie to sit down and have a drink and to not be angry. He testified that Austie said to Maggie, "Yes, Maggie, sit down and take a drink with us. I want to tell you something."[22]

Frank testified that Maggie flew into a rage, cursed at Austie, called her names, and threw a rolled ball of trash in her face. Maggie then jumped up and maneuvered around the chairs in the room, and, as that was happening, he saw a flash of something bright and heard the gun go off. He lunged at the gun, grabbed ahold of it, jerked it out of Austie's hand, and put it in his pocket. Frank stated he thought Maggie partly rose toward one of the chairs. He said she looked as though she was in a frenzy and noted that her "eyes bulged out of her head."[23]

Once Frank finished with his testimony and was cross-examined, he stepped down. The defense attorneys then called Austie to the stand. According to the March 8, 1894, edition of the *Weekly Pioneer Times*, she was startled and nervous as she rose and walked to the witness box. "Everyone in the courtroom was taken aback by the youthful appearance of the girl and by her childlike simplicity," the article noted. "Her testimony was given in the simple, hesitating way of a timid schoolgirl.[24]

She testified that she was sixteen years old, was born in Austria, that her parents resided in Crete, Nebraska, and that she left home going to Lincoln, Nebraska, last April. She stayed there until the latter part of last August, then she came to this city. . . . She first became acquainted with Maggie McDermott the day Maggie arrived back in town in November 1893. Austie told the court she had become involved with Frank DeBelloy the month before and that she'd only met Maggie once prior to the shooting. The two met at Maggie's room over Gib Stone's store.[25]

"On the day of the shooting, Frank came to the 400 about 4 o'clock," Austie explained, "and we went by the back way down the alley to the Mascott and entered the wine room by the back way. Frank ordered drinks, which were brought by Donovan, the bartender. We were in wine room No. 2. Frank and I talked for a while. I asked the bartender for some notepaper to write a note. After writing the note, I requested him to send it to room No. 3 at the Gib Stone building. Soon after that, Maggie McDermott and Hattie Rice came into the room.[26]

"Maggie, upon entering the room, looked at me and began calling me names. I was by Frank, and, as she advanced, I retired behind him. Frank said, 'Sit down, Maggie, and take a drink with us,' but she continued calling me vile names. I replied that 'I was no worse than she.' I then asked her to take a drink, then she began calling me names again and threw some paper she had in her hand in my face and jumped and grabbed a chair. I thought she was going to brain me, and I shot her. When she grabbed the chair, I was only a few feet away from her. She was going to kill me with the chair, and, because I was afraid she would do so I shot her. She was awful mad when she grabbed the chair. She looked so, and she talked so. She was lifting the chair up when I shot her."[27]

Upon being asked how long it was from the time Maggie lifted the chair to strike her and the time she fired the shot, Austie replied, 'Only a little bit of a time, a second.' Upon being told to take a chair and show how Maggie acted, she did so. She said she had her pistol in the bosom of her dress, which was a loose wrapper. Upon being told to show her motions in drawing the pistol, she took the pistol handed her and went through some motions, which she said she thought she did on the fatal day, but whether the same or not, she did not know positively, as on that day she was so excited, and was also scared to death of Maggie.[28]

Under cross-examination, Austie was asked why she had a gun with her. She told the court that she and Frank had planned to go hunting. Frank decided at the last minute that it was too damp and cold to go hunting and called off the outing. When asked to explain the two shots fired, Austie said that after the first shot had been fired Frank grabbed her arm and hand and attempted to wrench the gun from her, and in the scuffle the gun went off. As to her intentions in sending the note to Maggie to come to the saloon, the defendant said, "I had no ill feelings toward the girl. I wanted to talk to her and make up. She did not like me, and I knew it, and I wanted to tell her I did not like to have her talk about me. I was going to leave for Lincoln the next day, having telegraphed for a ticket, and I wanted to leave good friends with her."[29]

Closing arguments in the trial against Mary Yusta (Austie Trevyr) for the murder of Maggie McDermott were heard on Monday, March 12, 1894. Despite the sympathy the jury had for Austie given her young age, it did not allow sentiment to override its judgment. The teenager was found guilty, and she was sentenced to three years and seven months in the penitentiary in Sioux Falls. After Austie was sentenced for murder, Judge Plowman explained to her how the decision was reached:[30]

In this case I feel that I should say to you, Mary Yusta, that in the opinion of the court this jury has dealt with you with all the leniency that it was possible for a jury of men to do. The evidence in the case certainly would have warranted them in bringing in a verdict of murder and fixing the penalty at death, and on the record in this case, had such a sentence been rendered, I don't believe the board of pardons would have interfered with the decision of the death penalty. On account of your years and on account of your sex, this jury has taken it into their hands to render a verdict of manslaughter in the second degree.[31]

Your counsel has asked the court to send you to a reform school, and the court has carefully considered and thought of that in this case. If I could have found anything in the record which would justify me in sending you to reform school, and if I could have found anything in the record that would show that by sending you to reform school you could be reformed and brought back to a good citizen and a good woman, I would gladly send you there. But evidence shows you've been to reform school in Nebraska, and it seemed to have no effect upon you. You have left that and come here and gone into a life of shame and as I say, under the evidence, have committed a cold-blooded murder.[32]

No one but yourself and your God knows what you really intended. Whether you intended to take the life of Maggie McDermott, or whether you intended to take the life of Frank DeBelloy and then your own or not. The way the case was tried, it is evident that some things were brought out before the jury. Everything that would bear a merciful view of this case was brought out before the jury. Our reform school is intended for juveniles, and with the record of your conduct as you have disclosed it yourself upon the witness stand, I don't think I could conscientiously send you there among small children.[33]

In this case I have felt it my duty to give you the greatest sentence the law permits, and you may consider that on account of the mercy of the jury you have escaped with much less than you deserve.[34]

On January 4, 1897, Mary Yusta (aka Austie Trevyr), was discharged from the state penitentiary after completing the full sentence issued by the court. She returned to Deadwood and her old haunts at Belle Haskell's house. Some believed she returned to the 400 to resume her job as a prostitute, but she went back to minister to the soiled doves working there. By July 1897, Mary was on her way east to attend a seminary for young ladies. She wanted to learn about the Lord and share the Gospel to women at houses of ill repute.[35]

10

THE END FOR WOMEN OF EASY VIRTUE IN DEADWOOD

THE NATIONAL PROHIBITION ACT, COMMONLY KNOWN AS THE VOL-stead Act, was passed by Congress on January 16, 1919, and officially went into effect on January 17, 1920. A year after the Eighteenth Amendment was ratified, a national survey was conducted to chart the gains from a country free from drink. The survey revealed a significant reduction in poverty and crime. It also showed that family life had been enriched. "The front porch and the garden have come up as the corner saloon," the authors of the government survey noted. "Labor is more constant. Mondays are no longer blue or black. Absenteeism because of 'severe headaches' have decreased and industrial accidents likewise. Prohibition has all but emptied the county jails. Drinking is now very rare. Prostitution, too, has apparently greatly diminished and is on the verge of becoming non-existent."[1]

In 1921 in Deadwood, South Dakota, prostitution was nowhere near becoming "non-existent." Not every speakeasy in town had women of ill repute working there, but every bordello had liquor. The combination of both kept bawdy houses in the Black Hills busy. Many of Deadwood's earliest and most popular brothels such as the Gem Variety Theater and the Green Front Theater had been replaced with new houses in the Bad Lands area. Those establishments were named: Fern's Place, Rosie's Place, the Cozy Rooms, and the Bodega Rooms. The bordellos were all located above so-called respectable businesses. There were two distinct areas in those upstairs brothels: living quarters and a work section. The work sections were seldom open before noon.

Soiled dove known as Irene Love. One of many prostitutes working in Dead-wood at the turn of the century. COURTESY OF DEADWOOD HISTORY, INC. ADAMS MUSEUM COLLECTION, DEADWOOD, SD

Deadwood's main street, looking south from near the Fairmont Hotel in 1920. Prostitution continued to be a lucrative business in the Black Hills. COURTESY OF DEADWOOD HISTORY, INC. ADAMS MUSEUM COLLECTION, DEADWOOD, SD

Listed among bordello owners who competed for business in Deadwood in the 1920s and 1930s was a woman of German descent named Pauline Longland. Born Pauline Wirtz on May 22, 1891, in La Salle, Illinois, she came to South Dakota in 1910 and married Burr Longland in 1914.[2] Her bordellos were located at 616 and 618 Main Street. When she was arrested for running a disorderly house in August 1920 and paid a sixty dollar fine for the crime, the court warned her against further offenses. Pauline's line of work was so lucrative she wasn't inclined to leave the profession for any reason.[3]

On May 16, 1921, authorities raided her business, along with the businesses of several other bordello owners. She was taken into custody and charged with "keeping a house of ill fame." Between 1922 and 1930, she was arrested four more times for the same violation and three times for possessing and selling alcohol. In 1930, Pauline was sentenced to ninety days in jail on various liquor offenses and ninety days for maintaining a public nuisance.[4]

Pauline passed away on February 22, 1931, after suffering several months with a serious illness. "Her services, conducted by Rev. Alban Reed of St. Ambrose Catholic Church, were attended by a concourse of friends and relatives, and the casket was buried beneath a profusion of flowers in loving remembrance of the many friends of the deceased," the February 26, 1931, edition of the *Weekly Pioneer Times* read.[5]

Pauline was laid to rest at the St. Ambrose Catholic Church cemetery.[6]

Leaty Bell, better known as Gertrude Bell, was the proprietor of the Cozy Rooms. Born in Nebraska in 1884, she opened her business in 1928.[7] The brothel was upstairs from a laundry at 614 ½ Main Street. Prior to obtaining the house, she ran a place above a café and sold bootleg alcohol for which she was arrested several times. The first occasion happened on July 3, 1929, when federal prohibition enforcement officers staged a widespread liquor raid in Deadwood. Gertrude was among fourteen violators apprehended and charged with possession and sale of intoxicating liquor in violation of the National Prohibition Act. Prohibition ended in December 1933, and Gertrude was one of the first madams in town to submit an application to sell beer and wine.[8]

Two months after Gertrude began legally selling alcohol at her brothel, a customer named Wayne "Whitey" Copas assaulted her. Copas, a well-liked cook at the Main Street Café who had previously been arrested for keeping and storing liquor, tried to break into Gertrude's establishment on February 17, 1934. It was three o'clock in the morning when Copas arrived at the Cozy Rooms with two other men demanding to be let inside. When Gertrude refused his admittance, Copas became furious and started kicking the door. The madam finally relented and allowed the three to enter. The men were served a drink, and, when they finished their beers, they were asked to leave. Gertrude tried to escort them to the door, but Copas wasn't finished doing business at the brothel. He attacked Gertrude, punching her in the face and breaking her nose. The punch knocked her off feet, and, when she fell, she broke her arm.[9]

Copas was arrested for assault and battery. At his hearing, he testified that he was welcomed into Gertrude's place without trouble and told the court he had merely pushed her as she was attempting to kick him down the front steps. Copas was found guilty, sentenced to ten days in the city jail, and ordered to pay a fifty dollar fine.[10]

A similar situation occurred later that same year when musician Ned Bolger broke down the front door as he was leaving the Cozy Rooms. After visiting the brothel early Thanksgiving morning, he became angry with the woman he'd spent time with and tore the door off the hinges as he left the premises. Gertrude tried to stop him from storming off before he paid for the damages, but he refused. In court, he told the judge that he broke the door after being hit in the head with a blackjack and robbed of five dollars. Gertrude denied the allegation.[11]

On May 20, 1936, the largest raid conducted in the Black Hills since the late 1920s took place in Deadwood and Lead. Five madams, including Gertrude Bell, were apprehended for the illegal sale of high-grade alcohol. Gertrude and the owners of the other houses had licenses to sell a less potent beer (3.2% alcohol) only. They were arrested for possessing and selling massive quantities of whiskey and gin. The women each paid more than $200 in fines.[12]

Gertrude ran the Cozy Rooms successfully for more than ten years. When she passed away on November 21, 1941, at the age of sixty-three, the bordello was taken over by thirty-one-year-old Hazel Ione Fletcher. Hazel was more commonly known as Dixie.[13]

Prostitution was tolerated in the Black Hills but only to a point. Many believed it was a necessary evil, insisting respectable women were less likely to be harassed or raped as long as brothels were open. Women who willfully entered the profession were a curiosity, but young girls forced into such a life could not be allowed. More than thirty years after soiled dove Thelma Carpenter was charged by the federal government for violating the Mann Act and transporting women from state to state for immoral purposes, brothel owner Ellen Moore, alias Big Lu, was arrested in Deadwood for the same crime.[14]

Ellen Lucille Moore was born in Yankton, South Dakota, in 1918. The heavyset woman ran the Mecca bordello in Deadwood for a few years then moved to Forest Lake, Minnesota. It was there she became involved with one of the largest White slave rings in the history of the Northwest.[15]

Front façade of the Green Door brothel located at 618 Main Street in Dead-wood. SOUTH DAKOTA STATE HISTORICAL SOCIETY, SOUTH DAKOTA DIGITAL ARCHIVES, 2012-07-09-356

In February 1943, Big Lu and two other accomplices were appre-hended by FBI agents who caught them transporting girls from Min-nesota to Deadwood. Thirteen others were arrested in the raid. All were charged with violating the Mann Act. Big Lu was taken to a jail in St. Paul to stand trial. She was released from the Hennepin County jail on February 9, 1943, on a $2,500 bond. The nightly publicized trial ended in a conviction for Lu and her cohorts. She was sentenced to three years imprisonment.[16]

Over the next few years, politicians in Deadwood decided to seri-ously address the issue of prostitution in the city and finally enforce laws against the businesses that had been on the books for decades. On Octo-ber 6, 1949, Mayor Eddie Rypkema ordered the madams running "room-ing houses" in town to "close and discontinue their businesses." Those proprietors affected were Bea Wheeler from the Annex Rooms, Mickey Bruno from the Pine Rooms, and Hazel Fletcher from the Cozy Rooms. The women were warned that any violations would result in prosecution

Five soiled doves employed at Bea Wheeler's Annex Rooms pose for a group picture in 1940. COURTESY OF DEADWOOD HISTORY, INC. ADAMS MUSEUM COLLECTION, DEADWOOD, SD

to the fullest. "This is a move to eliminate houses of prostitution and the conditions that arise from them," Mayor Rypkema told reporters at the *Deadwood Pioneer Times*, "and also eliminate a certain element that question the enforcement of our laws."[17]

Hazel "Dixie" Fletcher wasn't intimidated by the local politicians' maneuverings. Prostitution had been a part of Deadwood for more than seventy years, and she wasn't convinced the Black Hills was finished with the trade. Hazel was born on May 4, 1902, in Rock Rapids, Iowa. She married Ross David Mills in Clear Lake, South Dakota, on August 13, 1921. The couple had two boys, and their marriage dissolved a few years after their second son was born in 1924. Ross took the children and moved to Minnesota while Hazel moved to Deadwood where she eventually became a madam.[18]

The obstinate woman acquired an off-sale liquor license in April 1948 and had every intention of utilizing what she'd paid for regardless of the Deadwood mayor's promise that "Deadwood will be the cleanest town

Madam Hazel "Dixie" Fletcher. COURTESY
OF DEADWOOD HISTORY, INC. ADAMS MUSEUM
COLLECTION, DEADWOOD, SD

in South Dakota when we get through."[19] The other bordello owners followed her lead. By January 1950, all the rooms were once again open for business.

Meanwhile, concerned citizens flooded Black Hills' newspapers with questions about soiled doves, their profession, and the possible benefits of legalizing the trade. Health officials were quick to respond to the queries with suggestions. "Would legalizing or controlling prostitution solve the venereal disease problem?" a Deadwood resident wrote and asked the director of the Pennington County Health Unit. "The idea behind this question is that a controlled activity could assure freedom from disease," the response to the question read. "This myth is firmly entrenched, but never has controlled prostitution lessened venereal infections."[20]

In late July 1951, government officials waged war against the brothel owners who refused to keep the doors of their houses closed. Law enforcement officers swept through the businesses on Friday evening, July 27, and more than twenty women were taken into custody.[21]

"The crackdown was directed at the Cozy Rooms, the Annex Rooms, Shasta Rooms, and the Pine Rooms on a complaint signed by Richard McGrath, Lawrence County sheriff," an article in the July 29, 1951, edition of the *Rapid City Journal* read.

State's attorney Richard Furze said Saturday following the multiple arraignment, 'The houses will remain closed, or there will be a repeat performance. They are a violation of the law and will not be tolerated.'[22]

Thirty-one warrants were issued, but only twenty-three women were apprehended.[23]

Moving in on the raids were members of the Lawrence County sheriff's office, agents from the attorney general's office, and the air police from Rapid City air force base.[24]

Madams and their employees were taken to the county jail and released under $1,000 bond each. Among those madams were Dixie Fletcher of the Pine Rooms, Nickie Bruno of the Cozy Rooms, and Bernice Wheeler of the Annex Rooms. . . . All the madams entered pleas of not guilty and were released under bond of $100 apiece.[25]

The madams arrested during the July raid appeared in court for sentencing on September 12, 1951. They had changed their pleas to guilty to avoid jail time, and each were ordered to pay fines of $300 and court costs that amounted to another $24.10 each.[26]

Citizens who felt the women were not adequately punished for their crimes made their sentiments known to newspaper reporters throughout the state. The September 19, 1951, edition of the *Mitchell Daily Republic* carried a story about the controversy.[27]

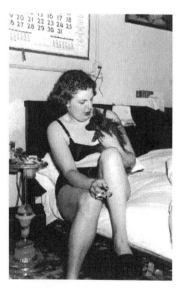

Deadwood is having difficulty in keeping houses of ill fame from operating within its borders. Attempts made at wiping out prostitution in Deadwood in the past have failed. The first vice crusade was in 1876. Several followed through the years. But little by little the brothels would return.[28]

As a result, some Deadwood businessmen feel that houses should be licensed and allowed to operate.[29]

Unnamed prostitute at Bea Wheeler's Annex Rooms. COURTESY OF DEADWOOD HISTORY, INC. ADAMS MUSEUM COLLECTION, DEADWOOD, SD

By the same token, it might be argued that, because robbers con-
tinue to steal despite arrests and jail terms, they should be given per-
mission to continue unhampered. The same might be said of traffic
violators, arsonists, embezzlers, and the like. It's regrettable, but it
seems, nevertheless, sure that there will always be propensity for crime
in some human beings, and that, this being the case, we will always
need vigilant law enforcement agencies and the courts to protect the
decent citizens from an extension of these activities.[30]

The same holds good for Deadwood. Sporadic "vice crusades,"
staged largely for political considerations, are not the answer to wip-
ing out that city's red-light district. The law will have to be ever vigi-
lant and ever strict in dealing with this riff-raff and, once they realize
that the authorities mean business and are no longer going to tolerate
their activities, they will take the hint and move on."[31]

Hazel Fletcher and her competitors continued to be unphased by
their recent run-ins with the law. Once the padlocks were removed from
the doors of the houses, customers arrived at the various rooms ready to
take up where they left off before the brothels were closed. Nine months
after authorities raided the businesses in July 1951, the police showed
up again. Shortly before midnight on June 19, 1952, state agents and
county law enforcement officers barged into the same four popular bordellos they'd visited in the past and arrested madams Beverly Gran, Kay
Gordon, Pat Cooper, and Hazel Fletcher. The women were charged with
keeping houses of ill repute, and their arraignments were scheduled for
June 21, 1952.[32]

According to the June 22, 1952, edition of the *Argus Leader*, "State's
attorney Richard Furze said some of the houses had been operating on
'calls' since the middle of April. He added that 15 to 20 prostitutes had
arrived, some during the past few days. Furze stated, 'We made a promise
to the citizens of Deadwood a year ago to protect them from all gambling and prostitution. We intend to keep it despite any rumors to the
contrary.'"[33]

The brothel owners were quickly bonded out, and preliminary hear-
ings began two months after their arrests. All but Hazel appeared in court

on September 11, 1952. She was seriously ill, and her case was postponed. Kay Gordon, Pat Cooper, and Beverly Gran were acquitted for lack of evidence. The charges against Hazel were dropped for the same reason on January 13, 1953.[34]

Madam Hazel Fletcher's liquor license was revoked in the summer of 1959. The lack of state authorization didn't stop her from selling alcohol at her brothel, having remained in continual operation since her acquittal six years prior. The flagrant disregard for the law prompted another raid. Lawmen again swooped down on Deadwood's shady businesses on October 15, 1959. Eighteen women were arrested and charged with operating houses of prostitution. Hazel was among them.[35]

"The women, some still clad in negligees, were fingerprinted and rushed through court proceedings," the October 16, 1959, edition of the *Argus Leader* reported.

Each asked for an attorney and posted $25 bond. Officers padlocked the doors at the Annex, Cozy, Shasta, and Pine Rooms—all upstairs over the businesses that line the picturesque main street of this historic mining town.[36]

Officers found at least thirty-five documents at the Shasta Rooms, signed and notarized by the girls that they had come to Deadwood of their own free will. This was an apparent attempt by the madams to skirt the Mann Act prohibiting interstate transportation of girls for immoral purposes.[37]

Officers also found about twenty-four fifths of liquor including a broken seal, timers and an elaborate collection box[38] *at the Shasta Rooms.*[39]

Eight or ten men were found in at least two of the places, and several others came during the course of the raids. Most were in their early twenties or late teens, and some gave Ellsworth Air Force Base addresses. Their names were taken, and they were released because South Dakota law does not provide for arresting men at bawdy houses.[40]

A permanent injunction against four women charged with conducting, operating, and maintaining houses of prostitution in Deadwood was ultimately granted. Hazel and the other professional women remained steadfast in their belief that customers would seek out their businesses regardless of the law and when they did the doors somehow would be open.[41]

Lawyers for the Deadwood brothel owners challenged the action of padlocking the houses, calling it improper. They argued that the women should have been served a summons but weren't. State's attorney William Carnahan had initiated the injunction and ordered the businesses padlocked saying the twenty-five-dollar fine provided under the law was not sufficient to protect the public morals.[42]

Given Hazel Fletcher's history of defying the law, it was only a question as to how long it would take before authorities acted on the rumor that she was still operating a brothel. In early January 1963, undercover criminal investigators visited two bordellos being run by Hazel. Agents Richard H. Meyer and James Moulds reported what occurred when they entered one of the businesses. The scene gave way to the charges that would follow.[43]

According to Meyer, both he and James were introduced to two women, and those women invited them to their rooms. Meyer asked one of the women why she wanted him to come to her room. "Now what in hell do you think for?" she replied. "Come on, I'm hot, and ready to go." Meyer asked how much the women charged and was told that ten dollars was the minimum. Moulds asked the women what it would cost to stay overnight and was told the price would be $200 or $300.[44]

The agents asked if they could have a drink first, and Hazel, who welcomed the men to the house, refused. She told them that "the city said we could run without whiskey and that is the way I'm going to run it." Meyer and Moulds excused themselves after the statement, telling Hazel they were going somewhere to drink and promised to return. The agents didn't return, however.[45]

More than a year passed before Hazel and Madams Bea Wheeler and Pat Cooper were ordered to appear in court after being arrested again for failure to comply with the permanent injunction against running houses of prostitution. The women stood trial for the offense on May 8, 1964. They were charged with contempt of court and fined $1,000 each and court costs of $8.80 each. Thirty-day jail sentences were suspended on condition that the fines and court costs be paid promptly and that the women comply with the injunction.[46]

Hazel kept herself out of the spotlight for several years after her arrest in 1964. The *Deadwood Pioneer Times* reported on the many times she was in and out of the hospital between December 1970 and October 1977.[47]

At the age of seventy-eight, Hazel was once again arrested for running a house of ill fame. More than fifteen women were arrested in a raid on four brothels on May 21, 1980. As they had for years, the four houses operated from the second floor of buildings in the 600 block of lower Main Street. The houses were distinguished by

Photograph of a four-drawer bureau taken as evidence in the raid on Pam Holliday's business in 1980. COURTESY OF DEADWOOD HISTORY, INC. ADAMS MUSEUM COLLECTION, DEADWOOD, SD

different colored doors and neon signs that read "Frontier Rooms," "Cozy Rooms," "Pine Rooms," and "Shasta Rooms." Anyone wanting to spend the evening with the women employed at the rooms could phone ahead for a meeting. The brothels were listed in the Yellow Pages of the local phone book. Hazel was one of six defendants named in a civil suit aimed at permanently closing brothels in Deadwood.[48]

Although the courts were dedicated to legally declaring the bordellos a nuisance, the public at large had mixed feelings about seeing the businesses go. Bordellos were a part of Deadwood's beginnings, and many feared the closure of the houses would mark the end of an era and that they would become merely a part of the town's fading Wild West history. Some legitimate businesses in downtown Deadwood believed the brothels should remain in operation because of their historic and monetary significance. Men who came to town to visit the brothels spent money at local restaurants and shops.[49]

When local authorities were asked by newspaper reporters at the *Argus Leader* in August 1979 why brothels were allowed to stay in business, the police chief replied, "We don't have a city ordinance against it." When he was reminded of the state law prohibiting prostitution, the police chief had no response. Some residents cited an old argument that the presence of prostitutes made the streets safer. Women employed as cooks or maids felt they could go home from work at any hour and not worry about being bothered by lecherous men. The feeling was that those types of men were being entertained elsewhere and, because of that, ladies could go about their lives without trouble. Whether for tourism, history, or safety concerns, prostitution had been accepted in Deadwood for ages.[50]

At a press conference in Rapid City on August 9, 1979, South Dakota governor William Janklow announced that houses of prostitution would be strictly dealt with under his watch. "I don't believe prostitution is a victimless crime," he told the public. "And it should not be legalized." The governor likened prostitutes to slaves and called their situations equally intolerable.[51]

Shortly after the court hearing for the soiled doves was set for June 1980, the issue of prostitution and the defendants arrested in the May raid were again the topic of discussion in the Black Hills. The madams were scheduled to appear at the hearing to plead their cases, and a group of concerned Deadwood citizens promised to be on hand as well to protest the women and their brothels. Those citizens circulated a petition against houses of ill repute and collected two hundred signatures urging the government to permanently close the bordellos.[52] Citizens in favor of allowing the doors of the brothels to stay open made their position known in telephone surveys conducted by the *Lead Daily Call* newspaper. The results showed that 43 percent of the people living in the Lead-Deadwood area wanted Deadwood's legendary brothels left alone.[53]

Black Hills residents representing both sides of the issue were present in the court room on June 17 when a motion to dismiss the civil complaint, filed by the state against individuals connected with the brothels, was denied.[54]

According to the June 17, 1980, edition of the *Lead Daily Call,*

Lawrence County Sheriff Charles Crotty and Deadwood Assistant Police Chief John Porter both testified at the hearing that establishments at 610 ½, 612 ½, 614 ½, and 616 ½ were houses of prostitution. Both Crotty and Porter admitted during cross examination by defense attorney John Fitzgerald that their offices had accepted gifts at Christmas time from the alleged prostitutes. Crotty said officers in the sheriff's office "probably have accepted bottles of booze at Christmas time."[55]

Porter said the Deadwood police officers, including Police Chief Robert Kelley, had accepted "one bottle from each of the houses," from the Spot Liquor Store in Deadwood in 1979. Porter said "other arrangements" were made for him to receive soft drinks because he doesn't drink.[56]

Both witnesses said they have received complains about the brothels, most saying that allowing prostitution is a double standard and accusing the department of accepting payoffs.[57]

The judge presiding over the matter scheduled the hearing for the civil suit for October. The legal paperwork outlining the case against Madam Fletcher was clear and to the point:

The State of South Dakota by and through Assistant General, James E. McMahon, Plaintiff, having made and presented to this court a duly verified complaint in writing, alleging that the defendant, Hazel Fletcher, also known as Dixie Fletcher, above-named is conducting, maintaining, and operating on the premises known as the Pine Rooms, 616 ½ Main Street, Deadwood, South Dakota, a house of prostitution. . . . The complaint prays the court that a permanent injunction be issued against the defendant, Hazel Fletcher, enjoining her from further conducting, maintaining, and operating said premises, on the grounds that the same is a public nuisance.[58]

The other women arrested in the May raid, and the owners of the building where the brothels were operated, were served documents with similar legal wording.[59]

In the weeks leading up to the trial, the brothels were ordered to be padlocked, and police were ordered to monitor the property to make sure no one tried to break the lock and resume business. Longtime Deadwood residents continued to voice their objections and support for the madams in newspapers throughout the region, and ministers in churches tailored their sermons around the controversial topic.

"Warning!" an advertisement for the Fellowship Baptist Church in the October 4, 1980, edition of the *Argus Leader* began,

> *Prostitution is still a heinous crime in the eyes of the Almighty God. Jesus said, "Whoremongers shall have their part in the lake which burneth with fire and brimstone, which is the second death," Rev. 21: 8. The Bible said, "Marriage is honorable in all, and the bed undefiled, but whoremongers and adulterers God will judge." Heb. 13:4. Again, "Be not deceived, neither fornicators, nor adulterers, nor sodomites shall inherit the kingdom of God," 1 Cor. 6:9, 10. Remember, "For by means of a whorish woman a man is brought to a piece of bread. . . . Can a man take fire in his bosom, and his clothes not be burned?" Prov. 6:26, 27. This Sunday's message "Deadwood: A Crime of Prostitution."[60]*

On October 7, 1980, Judge R. E. Brandenburg ruled that Deadwood's infamous houses of ill repute were public nuisances and instructed they be permanently closed. A dozen witnesses were called to the stand to testify that indeed, the brothels had been in operation for decades.[61]

Sheriff Charles Crotty told the court that a former state's attorney had prevented his office from raiding the brothels in the past and added that if they'd been allowed to do their job the houses might have become a thing of the past several years prior.[62]

In an interview conducted after the court had adjourned, Judge Brandenburg told reporters, "Everybody knew from the beginning what I was going to do. I had no choice. It's just very simple. I didn't hear any testimony that was opposed to it, so what else is there? It was just a matter of law that I got faced with deciding. There were no judgements of whether it's a good law or a bad law. It it's against the law, it's my job."[63]

Hazel Fletcher, Deadwood's oldest madam, left town in early 1981 and moved to Austin, Minnesota, where she passed away at the age of eighty-four on September 21, 1986.[64]

Outspoken brothel proprietor Pam Holliday, also known as Betty J. Campbell, madam of the Purple Door, shared her thoughts on prostitution at an open forum for the public at Deadwood's Franklin Hotel in late November 1980. "You're not going to stop prostitution by getting rid of women like Hazel Fletcher, Tommie Cox, and myself," Pam told citizens at the meeting. "The only thing I have control over is my body. The government owns the rest of me. A woman has the right to do with her body as she wishes.... They should legalize prostitution in Lawrence County."[65]

When the last soiled doves left town, it marked the end of bawdy houses in Deadwood. Like the notorious gunfighters, gamblers, and outlaws that were once a part of the town's wild beginnings, the profession faded into history.

11

THE LAST MADAM IN DEADWOOD

MORE THAN TWO DOZEN LAW ENFORCEMENT AGENTS WITH THE FED-
eral Bureau of Investigation, the South Dakota attorney general's office,
the United States Marshals Service, and two other criminal investigation
divisions congregated in Deadwood on the morning of May 21, 1980.
They arrived en masse at the popular brothel owned and operated by
Madam Pam Holliday. They'd been ordered to shut down her business,
and others like it, padlock the doors and arrest the women who worked
there. Thirteen prostitutes were taken into custody. Officers escorted the
courtesans down the stairs of the Purple Door to an awaiting van. Some
of the women wore pantsuits; some wore skirts and long shirts; all wore
high heels. They were quiet and followed directions with little fuss. The
crowd of townspeople who had gathered to watch the show were just
as quiet as the parade of soiled doves being led to the vehicle. Without
a word being spoken, the women were placed inside the van and then
hauled away.[1]

The onlookers stayed behind to witness the authorities load several
cardboard boxes filled with evidence collected from each of the bordellos into a rental truck. In addition to the boxes, a tall file cabinet with a
drawer labeled "receipts," a television, and a white desk with narrow slots
in a row in the back next to a pen affixed to the corner of the piece of furniture were lifted into the vehicle and secured tightly to the other items
with a bungee cord.[2]

By sunset, the rental truck and most of the law enforcement teams had
left the area. A few local police officers lingered behind to double-check

that the locks on the colorful entryways into the remaining four brothels in the infamous Wild West town were, indeed, tightly locked. The last prostitutes in Deadwood left town 104 years after the first prostitutes had arrived.[3]

When Pam Holliday arrived in the Black Hills in March 1969, at the urging of a friend, she was anxious to start work at the Cozy Rooms located at 614 ½ Main Street. Born Betty J. Campbell on June 9, 1931, in Lewiston, Montana, the future madam never imagined she'd pursue a career in prostitution. She was raised by her grandparents. Her grandfather was a sheriff in Jefferson County, Minnesota. She married a rancher and, in the beginning, was satisfied to be a wife and mother living on several hundred acres several miles southeast of Great Falls, Montana.[4]

Betty was the president of a social club for ranch wives called the Cowbelles and was a member of the PTA and 4-H Club. She also taught ceramics and painting at a local community center. Her world fell apart when she discovered her husband was having an affair. She left Montana and traveled to San Francisco with her two children and new boyfriend.

Madam Pam Holliday COURTESY OF DEADWOOD HISTORY, INC. ADAMS MUSEUM COLLECTION, DEADWOOD, SD

She struggled to find work, and it wasn't until a man offered her money in exchange for spending a moment with him that she realized she'd found her calling. She changed her name to Pam Holliday and never looked back.[5]

Pam returned to Montana after her boyfriend was arrested and imprisoned for selling stolen merchandise. She worked evenings as a prostitute and took care of her children during the day. She moved her family to Deadwood during the winter of 1969. By 1972, she'd established her own business known as the Frontier Rooms, later renamed the Purple Door. Between five and seven girls, ranging in ages from twenty-one to forty, were regularly in her employ. The brothel was usually open seven days a week, twenty-four hours a day. It was closed December 9 through January 6 every year so the staff could spend the holidays with their families.[6]

Madam Holliday always referred to her brothel as a "cat house" (slang for "prostitute") and boasted that her house was the best in town. She claimed to have the prettiest girls working for her and offered unique forms of entertainment for the men who visited her place. She had a

Madam Tommie Cox COURTESY OF DEADWOOD HISTORY, INC. ADAMS MUSEUM COLLECTION, DEADWOOD, SD

floor show featuring dancers and a trapeze act. Whenever the regular trapeze artist couldn't perform, Pam would take her place.[7]

By 1977, Pam had expanded her business holdings and was operating the Cozy Rooms, the brothel where she began her career in Deadwood. In July 1977, she was arrested for failure to file federal income taxes, an issue that would continue to plague her for years to come. She was fined $1,000 and placed on probation for the oversight for which she pled guilty.[8]

It was only a matter of time before authorities sought to charge her for operating a house of ill repute. The two other well-known madams in town, Hazel Fletcher and Tommie Cox, had been arrested numerous times on the same violation. The South Dakota attorney general's office wanted to put an end to the prostitution trade in Deadwood. Threats of jail time, fines imposed, and temporary injunctions weren't enough to make Pam and the other women quit the business.[9]

Pam was adamant that prostitution posed no threat to society and believed it should be legalized. "My house and others like it aren't harming the community," she told reporters in July 1980. "We're not on the street at night. We don't drag the men upstairs." According to the madam, 8 percent of the brothel's clientele were repeat customers. They were men who visited the bordello during the hunting season and motorcycle riders who gathered for the annual rally in Sturgis, thirteen miles away.[10]

In an interview with *Black Hills Monthly Magazine* in the summer of 1980, Pam happily supplied information about what it took to operate a brothel. She was usually awake all night managing the house and making sure the clients spent time with the women they requested. Her workday began at eight in the evening and lasted until 5:30 in the morning. Pam did not require that her employees offer references. Most of the women who worked for her were secretive about their backgrounds. There were rules of conduct all employees had to observe, and Pam spent a considerable amount of time enforcing those rules.[11]

"Number one, no drugs," Pam shared.

No pot, no pills, nothing. When they [her employees] went to the doctor and needed medication he would always call me first so I would know it was all right. I told them if they wanted to get messed up, take a vacation. Another rule was no profane language in the parlor. If you wanted to be treated like a lady, you must act like a lady. Keep your room clean at all times. No chewing gum.[12]

You've all watched television—Starsky and Hutch and Police-woman. When they portray a prostitute, what does she do? She's always chewing gum. It looks awful. Another rule, no food allowed in the rooms. If you and your "friend" cannot get along, call another girl.[13]

Rules of conduct while out in the community. Don't look right or left on the street. Now, if a gentleman speaks to them first, they will say hello, but I checked to see how they were dressed. I always make sure they look nice. The girls never stayed around town during off hours, and their working hours were up to them.[14]

Pam wasn't in Deadwood when the federal authorities raided the Purple Door. A friend informed her about what had occurred, and when she returned to town she was taken into custody and charged with "openly conducting, maintaining, and operating houses of prostitution." Pam hired Rapid City attorney John E. Fitzgerald Jr., to represent her in criminal court. His plan of attack was to challenge the federal government's accusation that the brothels were public nuisances and to dispute the idea that the businesses "injured the morality and reputation of Deadwood and the community of Lawrence County in general and offends decency." Fitzgerald insisted there wasn't sufficient grounds to establish the claim.[15]

The lawyer successfully established his position when he and Pam went before the judge overseeing the case on June 9, 1980. The temporary restraining order prohibiting Pam and the other madams from operating the houses of prostitution was lifted. Fitzgerald explained in court that a nuisance complaint specifically dealing with houses of prostitution could only be brought by the state's attorney or a private citizen of the county. The state's attorney promised to refile with the county cosigning.[16]

Pam's Purple Door was located above the Beer Barrel Bar on Main Street. COURTESY OF DEADWOOD HISTORY, INC. ADAMS MUSEUM COLLECTION, DEADWOOD, SD

A second temporary restraining order to keep the brothels closed was quickly issued. The action left Pam with no regular source of income and no funds to pay for her defense. She was left with no other choice but to liquidate her business and try to sell the items left in the brothel after the FBI took what they needed as evidence.[17]

A public auction was held on July 17, 1980, and the furnishings, appliances, and decorative pieces at Pam's Purple Door were presented to sell. In addition to the many interested shoppers hoping to buy lamps, parlor couches, and nightstands, there was a group of respectable women who objected to closing the bordellos who congregated at the scene. They wore dance hall costumes and carried placards that read, "Bring back our girls."[18]

Several of the Purple Door's furnishings sold for as little as $5. Two purple ashtrays sold for $50 each, a mirror went for more than $100, and knick-knacks brought $8 to $20 each.[19]

Pam had the brightly colored purple door leading to the brothel removed and donated it to the Pioneer Auto Museum in Murdo, South Dakota.[20]

The official ending of prostitution and the closing of the brothels in the infamous Western community made national news. Network news producers, the host of the *Today Show*, and Phil Donahue sought interviews with Pam about her profession and the end of a colorful era.[21]

The former madam remained in the public eye after the auction ended, participating in a panel discussion in November 1980 about the history of prostitution in Deadwood. The four other members of the panel consisted of a reverend, two college professors, and an attorney. "We're not going to get rid of prostitution by getting rid of Pam and closing the brothels," the madam told the audience attending the event. "I'm not ashamed of anything I've done. If I had it to do over again, I'd start at sixteen, and by twenty-one I'd own all of Deadwood, or at least, part of it," she added.[22]

Pam left Deadwood for Rapid City where she opened a bar called Pam's Other Door. While awaiting trial on another set of charges for income tax evasion, coercion, and enticement of a female for prostitution, she served drinks to patrons in the community. The occasional customer who recognized her and knew of her former job would ask if she was still involved in the trade. She assured them she only sold liquor and would never go back to the life she once had. "If someone wanted to start a house, I'd help them," she admitted in an article for the *Black Hills Monthly Magazine*, "but as far as me going back . . . never."[23]

Almost two years after the Purple Door was closed, Pam Holliday appeared before the judge and pled guilty to interstate transportation of women for the purposes of prostitution and evading federal income taxes in 1976. She was fined $5,000 on the interstate transportation charge and was placed on five years of probation. As part of the probation, she swore to obey all laws and "completely disassociate herself from prostitution." The sentence for the tax evasion conviction wasn't as lenient. Pam was sentenced to four years in federal prison and fined $5,000.[24]

When Pam was released from prison in 1986, she moved to St. Michael, Minnesota, to be near her daughter and grandchildren. She died of natural causes on July 25, 2003, at the Hospice Facility in Brooklyn Center, Minnesota. She was seventy-two years old when she passed away.[25]

Madam Pam Holliday's Deadwood cathouse burned to the ground on February 15, 1982.[26]

12

Business in the Bad Lands

Houses of prostitution were in operation in Deadwood for more than a hundred years. The following is a directory of the most popular houses in the Black Hills, the address of the houses, their owners, and their encounters with the law.

Main thoroughfare of Deadwood in 1900. COURTESY OF LIBRARY OF CONGRESS

ACE HIGH ROOMS

Proprietors: Frank Mitchell and Inez Keough, 1932–1934

Proprietress: Languare Mook, 1934–1935. Born in South Dakota in 1904. Married to Harold Mook[1]

Proprietress: Alice Copperman, 1935–1936. Born in Norway in 1913. Married to M. J. "Curley" Copperman, fight promoter and owner of the Virginia Rooms[2]

Proprietress: Delphine Shultz, 1936

Address: 612 ½ Main Street, Deadwood, South Dakota

Arrests/Legal Notices

December 7, 1932: Owners Mitchell and Keough taken into custody and charged with selling intoxicating liquor.[3]

November 4, 1934: Brothel broken into and $250 stolen from cash box. Three men were arrested and prosecuted for the crime.[4]

February 1936: Business closed.[5]

ARCADE ROOMS

Proprietress: Iva Ginter. Born 1890. Married to a carpenter named Ase Ginter. The couple and their three children lived on William Street in Deadwood, South Dakota.[6] Iva was granted a divorce from Ase in 1935 on the grounds of conviction of a felony. Ase was sent to the state penitentiary at Sioux Falls for grand larceny.[7]

Address: 616½ Main Street, Deadwood, South Dakota

Earliest recorded mention of Arcade Rooms is from August 1891.[8]

Arrests/Legal Notices

July 4, 1929: Madam Ginter charged with violating national prohibition laws.[9]

September 12, 1941: Clyde Purcell and Jean Collins charged with vagrancy.[10]

March 1943: Business closed.[11]

ANNEX ROOMS

Proprietress: Madam Berniece "Bea" Wheeler. Born March 15, 1912, in Deadwood. Owned a two-room house on Railroad Avenue.[12]

Addresses: 664 ½ Main Street and 658 ½ Main Street, Deadwood, South Dakota

Arrests/Legal Notices

October 13, 1949: Notice to refrain from illegal operations issued by Mayor Eddie Rypkema; Madam Wheeler ordered to adhere strictly to the privileges granted in the rooming house and nonintoxicating liquor licenses as issued by the city council.[13]

July 27, 1951: Madam Wheeler arrested and charged with keeping a house of ill fame.

Prostitutes working in the rooms and arrested and fined $25.00 for violation along with $15.10 court costs were Betty Herring, Ginger Ward, Ann Jenks, and Ruby Russell.[14]

June 20, 1952: Beverly Gray, acting as madam in Bea Wheeler's temporary absence, was arrested and charged with keeping a house of ill fame. She spent the night in jail and was released on $2,000 bond.[15]

October 15, 1959: Sally Black, acting as madam in Bea Wheeler's temporary absence was arrested and charged with conspiracy to commit the felony of keeping a house of ill fame.[16]

Prostitutes working in the rooms and arrested were Sally Black, Jean Taylor, Catherine Keil, and Michelle Miller.[17]

October 30, 1959: Madam Bea Wheeler charged with keeping a house of ill fame and order stand trial for offense.[18]

September 27, 1960: A permanent injunction against the house of ill fame (Annex Rooms) located at 664 ½ Main Street was granted in court.[19]

January 1963: Madam Wheeler continues with the business at the Annex Rooms 658 ½ Main Street location.

April 19, 1964: Civil action filed against Madam Wheeler for contempt of a permanent court injunction to cease conducting, maintain and operating a house of prostitution.[20]

May 8, 1964: Madam Wheeler is found in contempt of injunction and fined $1,000 along with $8.80 in court costs.[21]

May 1964: Annex Rooms at both locations closed.

COZY ROOMS

Proprietress: Gertrude Bell, 1932–1941

Proprietress: Hazel "Dixie" Fletcher, 1941–1950

Proprietress: Pearl Marie Melton (aka Mickey Bruno), 1951–1969. Born in Missouri in 1886.[22]

Coproprietress: Mary Putnam (aka Kay Gordon), 1952–1953. Sold her interest in brothel but served as manager of business until 1957.[23]

Coproprietress: Barbara Lee McMillen, 1960–1969, Sole Proprietress 1970–1977

Address: 614½ Main Street, Deadwood, South Dakota

Arrests/Legal Notices

February 20, 1934: Madam Bell attacked by Wayne "Whitey" Copas. Copas was arrested for assault and battery.[24]

May 21, 1934: Madam Bell arrested and charged with selling intoxicating liquor without a license.[25]

October 6, 1949: Madam Bell ordered by Deadwood authorities to close business.[26]

July 27, 1951: Madam Bruno taken into custody and charged with keeping a house of ill fame.[27]

Prostitutes working in the rooms arrested and fined $25.00 for violation along with $15.10 court costs were Barbara Evans and Shirley Snyder.[28]

June 20, 1952: Madam Kay Gordon taken into custody and charged with running a house of prostitution. Released on a $2,000 bond.[29]

October 15, 1959: Brothel manager Barbara McMillen charged with operating a house of ill fame.[30] Prostitutes working in the rooms and arrested were Pat Kelley, Karen Wilson, Gigi Ladiea, and John Murphy.[31]

December 22, 1959: Madam Bruno's beer license revoked by the State Alcoholic Beverage Division.[32]

September 27, 1960: A permanent injunction against the house of ill fame (Cozy Rooms) located at 614 ½ Main Street was granted.

March 30, 1965: Madam Bruno and brothel robbed by Richard P. Heddon.[33]

April 13, 1967: Madam Bruno, prostitute Shirley Larson, and brothel robbed by two assailants.[34]

DALY ROOMS

Proprietress: Martha Jones Daly

Address: 610 ½ Main Street, Deadwood, South Dakota

Arrests/Legal Notices

January 26, 1932: Madam Daly charged with violating federal prohibition laws by selling intoxicating liquor.[35]

April 16, 1932: Madam Daly taken into custody and charged with sale, possession, and keeping and storing intoxicating liquor.[36] She was fined and served a three-month sentence at the Lawrence County jail. Daly sold her business after she was released on August 17, 1932.[37]

FRONTIER ROOMS

Proprietress: Betty June Campbell (aka Pam Holliday), 1972–1980, Born on June 9, 1931 in Lewiston, Montana.[38] Died on July 25, 2003 in Hennepin, Minnesota[39]

Address: 614½ Main Street, Deadwood, South Dakota

MECCA ROOMS

Proprietress: Ellen Lucille Moore (alias Big Lu)

Address: 664 ½ Main Street, Deadwood, South Dakota

Arrests/Legal Notices

February 2, 1943: Madam Moore charged and jailed for violating the Mann Act, which prohibits the transportation of women in interstate commerce for immoral purposes.[40]

February 1943: Business closed.[41]

NIFTY ROOMS

Proprietor: Charlie Brown, 1933–1936

Proprietress: Rebecca Havens, 1936–1951

Married to William Havens an odd job laborer. The couple had five children. William died in a hit and run accident in 1941.[42]

Address: 640 ½ Main Street, Deadwood, South Dakota

Recognized as the "best whorehouse in Deadwood" by Judge R. E. Brandenburg. "There was a line of guys up the stairway every weekend," he noted in 1982 when he ordered the house of ill repute closed.[43]

Arrests/Legal Notices

May 21, 1936: Owner Brown charged with selling liquor by the drink without a license.[44]

February 1951: Business closed.[45]

PHOENIX ROOMS

Proprietress: Geraldine Murphy Born in Utah in 1911.[46]

Address: 679 Main Street, Deadwood, South Dakota

Arrests/Legal Notices

May 7, 1935: Madam Murphy issued 3.2 percent beer license for establishment.[47]

July 2, 1935: Madam Murphy ordered by Sheriff E. E. Minard to cease operations of establishment on the grounds that it is a public nuisance.[48]

November 1935: Building sold and the business closed.

PINE ROOMS

(Formerly the Arcade Rooms)

Proprietress: Hazel "Dixie" Fletcher, 1948–1949, 1951–1980

Proprietress: Pearl Marie Melton (aka Mickey Bruno), 1949–1950. Born in Missouri in 1886.[49]

Address: 616 ½ Main Street, Deadwood, South Dakota

Arrests/Legal Notices

October 6, 1949: Madam Bruno ordered by Deadwood authorities to close business.[50]

July 28, 1951: Madam Fletcher was charged with keeping a house of ill fame.[51]

Prostitutes working in the rooms and arrested were Vickie Turner, Jerry Jerome, Jacki Carroll, and Mickie Summers.[52]

June 21, 1952: Madam Fletcher taken into custody and charged with keeping a house of ill repute.[53]

October 15, 1959: Madam Fletcher taken into custody and charged with keeping a house of ill repute.[54]

Prostitutes working in the rooms and arrested were Judy Evans, Laverta (Babe) Snell, Boots Smith, and Ann Scott.[55]

September 27, 1960: A permanent injunction against the house of ill fame (Pine Rooms) located at 616 ½ Main Street was granted.[56]

April 17, 1964: Madam Fletcher held in contempt for not adhering to a court order to close the Pine Rooms brothel. She was fined $1,000 for the violation and $8.80 in court costs.[57]

SHASTA ROOMS

(Formerly the Daly Rooms and Winner Rooms and later known as the Beige Door and operated by Tommy Cox)

Proprietress: Cora Reid, 1936–1936, 1938–1946

Proprietor: Mike Kelley, 1937–1938

Proprietress: Myrtle "Mert" O'Hara, 1947–1951

Proprietress: Pat Cooper, 1952–1964

Address: 610 ½ Main Street, Deadwood, South Dakota

Arrests/Legal Notices

May 20, 1936: Madam Reid taken into custody and charged with illegal sale of liquor.[58]

January 2, 1938: Owner Mike Kelley charged with disturbing the peace at the brothel. Order to pay a five dollar fine.[59] Charge was brought on by a customer named Parks DuPont. DuPont discharged a firearm during an argument at the brothel. He was arrested and sentenced to ten days in jail.[60]

January 11, 1939: Customer named Lodell Jay taken into custody and charged with assault and battery after beating Madam Reid and creating a disturbance at the brothel.[61]

July 27, 1951: Brothel raided. Madam O'Hara not at house when police arrived and a warrant was issued for her arrest. Soiled doves working in the rooms and arrested and fined $25.00 for prostitution along with $15.10 court cost were Billie Douglas also known as Sandy Anderson, Gale Scott, Betty Myers, Tony Ballenger, Judy Allen, and Dee Brownell.[62]

August 7, 1951: Madam O'Hara taken into custody and charged with operating a house of ill repute. She was fined $300 and sentenced to a year in prison.[63]

June 20, 1952: Madam Cooper taken into custody and charged with keeping a disorderly house.[64]

October 15, 1959: Madam Cooper taken into custody and charged with keeping a house of ill fame and selling liquor without a license.[65]

September 27, 1960A permanent injunction against the house of ill fame (Shasta Rooms) located at 610 ½ Main Street was granted.[66]

April 17, 1964: Madam Cooper held in contempt for not adhering to a court order to close the Shasta Rooms brothel. She was fined $1,000 for the violation and $8.80 in court costs.[67]

SHY-ANN ROOMS

Proprietress: Jackie Burke, March 1936–May 1936

Proprietress: Beatrice Westover, 1936–1937. Born in 1910.[68] Attempted suicide on March 29, 1936. Transported to St. Joseph Hospital where she made a full recovery.[69] Seriously injured in car accident on August 3, 1936. Transported to St. Joseph Hospital where she made a full recovery.[70]

Proprietor: Pat Welch 1937–1939

Address: 612½ Main Street, Deadwood, South Dakota

Arrests/Legal Notices

May 21, 1936: Madam Burke taken into custody and charged with engaging in the on-sale (by the drink) sale of intoxicating liquor without a state license. Fined $40 and court costs of $10.10.[71]

August 27, 1937: Patron Ted Welch punched prostitute Winifred Arndt and she retaliated by hitting him in the head with a club. Welch was taken into custody and charged with disorderly conduct. His injuries were treated by a physician at the jail.[72]

October 11, 1937: Brothel owner and operator Pat Welch was taken into custody after beating one of the prostitutes in his employ. He was sentenced to ten days in the county jail and assessed the cost of the case after pleading guilty to the charge of assault and battery.[73]

November 1942: Brothel sold and subsequently closed.[74]

THE THREE NICKELS
Proprietress: Billy Baldwin

Address: 555 Main Street, Deadwood, South Dakota

Recognized as one of the oldest brothels in town.[75]

VIRGINIA ROOMS
Proprietor: M. J. "Curley" Cooperman

Address: 606 ½ Main Street, Deadwood, South Dakota

Arrests/Legal Notices

May 20, 1936: Owner Cooperman taken into custody and charged with engaging in the on-sale (by the drink) of intoxicating liquor without a state license.[76]

April 1938: Virginia Rooms closed. Cooperman was a fight promoter, and his business was used strictly as a venue for boxing matches. Prostitutes who visited the matches to solicit clients were acting on their own behalf.[77]

WINNER ROOMS

(Formerly the Daly Rooms)

Proprietress: Vivian Piper, 1932–1933

Proprietor: Harry Gardner, 1933–1934

Proprietor: Marvin Huntley, 1934–1935

Address: 610 ½ Main Street, Deadwood, South Dakota

Arrests/Legal Notices

October 29, 1932: Madam Piper taken into custody for possession of moonshine liquor.[78]

June 4, 1933: Soiled dove Catherine LaDeaux attempts to kill herself with an overdose of veronal. The former Montana resident was taken to St. Joseph hospital.[79]

May 7, 1934: Winner Rooms' bartender "Sailor" Huntley was taken into custody and charged with assault and battery for beating a customer named Perry Willeford.[80]

July 7, 1934: Winner Rooms' owner Marvin Huntley taken into custody and charged with operating gambling games and gambling apparatuses. He was later fined $100 and sentenced to thirty days in jail.[81]

October 16, 1934: Soiled dove Lavinia Lamm taken into custody and charged with grand larceny. Customer accused Lamm of stealing thirty-five dollars from him. Marvin Huntley was charged with assault for smacking the customer down when he protested the theft.[82]

BEIGE DOOR

(Formerly the Shasta Rooms)

Proprietress: Elsie L. Irwin (also known as Tommie/Tommy Cox), 1969–1980. Born on February 9, 1922, in Haming Falls, West Virginia.[83] Died on June 14, 1989, at the age sixty-seven.

Address: 610 ½ Main Street, Deadwood, South Dakota

Arrests/Legal Notices

May 21, 1980: Madam Cox charged with operating a house of prostitution and a permanent injunction was filed to shut business down.[84]

October 9, 1980: Permanent injunction to close the brothel was granted.[85]

PURPLE DOOR

(Formerly the Cozy Rooms and Frontier Rooms)

Proprietress: Betty June Campbell (aka Pam Holliday), 1977–1980. Born on June 9, 1931, in Lewiston, Montana.[86] Died on July 25, 2003, in Hennepin, Minnesota.[87]

Address: 614½ Main Street, Deadwood, South Dakota

Arrests/Legal Notices

May 21, 1980: Madam Holliday charged with operating a house of prostitution and a permanent injunction was filed to shut business down.[88]

October 9, 1980: Permanent injunction to close the brothel was granted.[89]

GREEN DOOR AND WHITE DOOR

(Formerly the Pine Rooms)

Proprietress: Hazel "Dixie" Fletcher, 1969–1980

Address: 616 ½ Main Street, Deadwood, South Dakota

Arrests/Legal Notices

May 21, 1980: Madam Fletcher charged with operating a house of prostitution and a permanent injunction was filed to shut business down.[90]

October 9, 1980: Permanent injunction to close the brothel was granted.[91]

AFTERWORD

WHEN THE BROTHEL KNOWN AS THE BEIGE DOOR REOPENED IN DEAD-wood in the summer of 2020, patrons followed a tour guide, instead of a prostitute, into each bedroom. The Deadwood Historic Preservation Commission, the Main Street Initiative Committee, and Deadwood History, Inc. (DHI) developed the idea of opening the only brothel tour in the Black Hills in 2017. DHI, which oversees the museum where the Shasta Rooms/Beige Door once was, and is now known as The Brothel Deadwood, is a nonprofit organization. They are also in charge of four other properties in Deadwood: the Adams Museum, the Days of '76 Museum, the Historic Adams House, and the Homestake Adams Research and Cultural Center. Prior to moving forward with the unique way of recognizing the bawdy history of the town's busy red-light district, the staff at DHI presented the idea to the community to determine the interest in the project. Most of the residents were in favor of the venture.

Nugget, LLC is the owner of the building where The Brothel Deadwood is located. The company managed and financed the rehabilitation work done on the second floor of the structure where the soiled doves conducted business. Federal authorities raided the notorious brothel location and three others like it in May 1980. More than a dozen women were arrested at that time and charged with practicing the world's oldest profession. A judge subsequently ordered the brothels permanently shut down.

Carolyn Weber, executive director of DHI and several staff members at the organization devoted countless hours to researching the details of the business to create a setting that correctly depicts life in the brothel. The rooms are curated with a variety of period-appropriate furnishings that reflect the 104-year history of prostitution in Deadwood.

According to Weber, "The Brothel Deadwood has had a steady flow of visitors since the tour opened." She explained that people aren't surprised to know that prostitution was widespread in the early days of Deadwood's founding but are taken aback to learn that as many as eight women per brothel worked in the trade until 1980. "They made a good living because of the location of their businesses," Weber shared. "There were men from all walks of life in the Black Hills for many decades. There were miners, ranchers, loggers, railroaders, military. Women saw an opportunity to meet the needs of the men in the region, capitalized on it, and some of them profited substantially."

Laws against prostitution in South Dakota were on the books for decades before authorities finally shut the trade down in Deadwood. Citizens there knew the business existed, but few talked about it in polite company. It was "an open secret." The Brothel Deadwood pays homage to that open secret.

The Brothel Deadwood is located at 610 Main Street in Deadwood, South Dakota. For more information phone (605) 559-0231 or visit deadwoodhistory.com and deadwoodbrothel.com.

NOTES

INTRODUCTION

1. The June 8, 1876, edition of the *Deadwood Pioneer Times* notes that Phatty's last name was Thomas. Deadwood History, Inc. indicates that his last name was Thompson.

2. *Deadwood Pioneer Times*, June 8, 1876.

3. Ibid.

4. Chris Enss, *Wicked Women: Notorious, and Wayward Ladies from the Old West* (Guilford, CT: TwoDot Books, 2015), IX.

5. *Deadwood Pioneer Times*, June 8, 1876.

6. Ibid.

7. Ibid.

8. Enss, *Wicked Women*, XI.

9. *Daily Champion*, June 9, 1877.

10. *Funk & Wagnalls New Encyclopedia*, Vol. 9, 1973.

11. *Black Hills Champion*, August 27, 1877.

12. *Press and Daily Dakotaian*, October 16, 1877.

13. *The Nebraska State Journal*, February 22, 1877.

14. Ibid.

15. Ibid.

16. *Daily Champion*, June 9, 1877.

17. A class of women considered to be of doubtful morality and social standing.

18. Ibid.

19. A reference to men who paid women for sex.

20. *The Black Hills Daily Times*, June 13, 1878; *The Black Hills Daily Time*, August 27, 1877.

21. *The Black Hills Weekly Times*, October 14, 1877.

22. *Frank Leslie's Weekly*, September 11, 1877.

23. Ibid.

24. Ibid.; *The Black Hills Champion*, August 27, 1877.

25. *The Black Hills Weekly Pioneer*, March 17, 1877; *Press and Dakotaian*, June 26, 1877; *The Black Hills Weekly Pioneer*, April 10, 1880; *The Black Hills Weekly Journal*, April 2, 1881.

26. *The Black Hills Daily Times*, May 20, 1881.

27. Ibid.

28. Ibid.

29. Ibid.

30. *Argus Leader*, April 8, 1895; *The Daily Deadwood Pioneer Times*, October 21, 1890.

31. *The Black Hills Union*, August 14, 1891.

32. *The Daily Plainsman*, September 22, 1892.

33. *The Black Hills Daily Times*, December 11, 1892.

34. *The Black Hills Weekly Times*, December 17, 1892.

35. Ibid., January 7, 1893.

36. *The Weekly Pioneer Times*, March 9, 1893; *The Black Hills Weekly Times*, June 17, 1893.

37. *The Black Hills Weekly Times*, April 27, 1895; *The Black Hills Daily Times*, August 19, 1894.

38. *The Black Hills Daily Times*, September 21, 1895; *The Black Hills Weekly Times*, June 8, 1895.

39. *Deadwood Evening Independent*, October 2, 1895.

40. *The Black Hills Weekly Herald*, July 27, 1886.

41. *The Black Hills Daily Times*, September 15, 1889.

42. Ibid.

43. Ibid.

44. *The Black Hills Weekly Times*, September 26, 1896.

45. Ibid.

46. Ibid.

47. *The Daily Deadwood Pioneer Times*, May 6, 1902.

48. Ibid., January 31, 1900.

49. *The Weekly Pioneer Times*, March 6, 1902.

50. Ibid.

51. Ibid.

52. *The Daily Deadwood Pioneer Times*, September 28, 1905.

53. Ibid.

CHAPTER 1

1. *Daily Champion*, June 14, 1877.

2. *The Black Hills Weekly Pioneer*, May 26, 1877; Jerry L. Bryant and Barbara Fifer, *Deadwood's Al Swearingen: Manifest Evil in the Gem Theatre* (Helena, MT: FarCountry Press, 2018), 11–13.

3. *Deadwood's Al Swearingen*, 1–5, 11–13.

4. Ibid., 9–11.

5. Ibid.

6. *The Black Hills Weekly Pioneer Times*, April 21, 1877.

7. *The Black Hills Daily Times*, December 12, 1877.

8. *The Black Hills Daily Times*, December 26, 1877.

9. Ibid.

10. John S. McClintock and Edward L. Seen, *Pioneer Days in the Black Hills: Accurate History and Facts Related By One of the Early Day Pioneers* (Norman: University of Oklahoma Press, 2000), 69–70.

11. Ibid., 82–83; Michael Trump, *Raiding Deadwood's Bad Lands: It's Illegal History of Prostitution and Gambling* (Deadwood, SD: The Adams Museum & House, Inc., 2009), 25–26.

12. *The Black Hills Weekly Times*, August 19, 1877; *Adams Banner* Vol. 5 , No. 4 Fall 2004.

13. *The Daily Deadwood Pioneer Times*, June 25, 1878.

14. *Adams Banner* Vol. 5, No. 4 Fall 2004.

15. *Bismarck Weekly*, August 7, 1878; *The Black Hills Daily Times*, August 2, 1878; Bryant and Fifer, *Deadwood's Al Swearingen*, 88–89.

16. *The Daily Deadwood Pioneer Times*, December 18, 1879.

17. "Al Swearingen & the Notorious Gem Theater," Legends of America, November 2021, www.legendsofamerica.com/we-gemsaloon/; *The Black Hills Daily Times*, May 19, 1877.

18. *The Black Hills Daily Times*, June 10, 1877.

19. Chris Enss, *Wicked Women: Notorious, and Wayward Ladies from the Old West* (Guilford, CT: TwoDot Books, 2015), 9–11.

20. Ibid.

21. Ibid.

22. Ibid., 11–13

23. Ibid.

24. *The Black Hills Daily Times*, December 7, 1877.

25. Ibid.

26. *The Black Hills Weekly Times*, December 4, 1877.

27. *Press and Daily Dakotaian*, September 26, 1879.

28. *The Black Hills Daily Times*, June 27, 1879.

29. *Adams Banner* Vol. 5 No. 4 Fall 2004; *The Black Hills Daily Times*, October 5, 1879; *The Daily Deadwood Pioneer Times*, December 31, 1879.

30. *The Weekly Pioneer Times*, January 1, 1880.

31. *The Black Hills Daily Times*, January 1, 1880.

32. *The Weekly Pioneer Times*, January 22, 1880; *Adams Banner* Vol. 5 No. 4 Fall 2004; *The Black Hills Daily Times*, October 5, 1879.

33. *The Black Hills Daily Times*, January 20, 1880; *The Weekly Pioneer Times*, January 22, 1880.

34. *The Black Hills Daily Times*, December 28, 1879.

35. Ibid., January 20, 1880.

36. *Press and Daily Dakotaian*, February 26, 1880; *The Black Hills Daily Times*, February 22, 1880.

37. *The Black Hills Daily Times*, May 26, 1880; *The Weekly Pioneer Times*, June 9, 1880.

38. *The Black Hills Daily Times*, May 26, 1880.

39. Ibid.

40. *The Weekly Pioneer Times*, June 9, 1880.

41. *The Black Hills Weekly Times*, November 27, 1880.

42. *The Black Hills Daily Times*, March 30, 1880.

43. *The Weekly Pioneer Times*, May 29, 1880.

44. *The Black Hills Daily Times*, June 1, 1880; *The Black Hills Daily Times*, June 2, 1880.

45. *Adams Banner* Fall 2005.

46. Ibid.

47. *The Black Hills Daily Times*, May 8, 1881.

48. Ibid.; *Adams Banner* Fall 2005.

49. *The Black Hills Daily Times*, October 17, 1881.

50. Ibid.

51. Ibid., November 6, 1883.

52. *The Daily Deadwood Pioneer Times*, November 7, 1883.

53. *The Black Hills Daily Times*, April 29, 1884; *Adams Banner* Spring 2006.

54. *The Black Hills Daily Times*, September 5, 1884.

55. Ibid.

56. Ibid.

57. The Daily Deadwood Pioneer Times, December 21, 1886; *The Black Hills Daily Times*, August 18, 1887.

58. *The Black Hills Daily Times*, September 2, 1887.

59. Ibid.

60. Ibid.

61. *The Weekly Pioneer Times*, April 5, 1894.

62. Bryant and Fifer, *Deadwood's Al Swearingen*, 105; *The Weekly Pioneer Times*, April 5, 1894.

63. *The Weekly Pioneer Times*, April 5, 1894.

64. Ibid.

65. *The Black Hills Daily Times*, September 18, 1894.

66. *The Black Hills Daily Times*, March 20, 1895.

67. Ibid.

68. Ibid.

69. Ibid.

70. *Rapid City Journal*, December 31, 1903; *The Herald*, November 24, 1904.

71. *The Herald*, November 24, 1904.

CHAPTER 2

1. *Rapid City Journal*, March 3, 1997; *Oakland Tribune*, December 16, 1928.

2. Chris Enss, *Wicked Women: Notorious, and Wayward Ladies from the Old West* (Guilford, CT: TwoDot Books, 2015), 61.

3. Ibid.

4. Ibid.

5. Ibid.

6. Ibid.

7. Ibid.

8. Ibid.

9. Ibid.

10. Ibid.

11. Ibid.

12. Ibid.
13. Ibid.
14. Ibid.
15. Ibid.
16. Ibid.
17. Ibid.
18. *The Bodie Daily Free Press*, September 8, 1879.

CHAPTER 3

1. *Press and Daily Dakotaian*, July 10, 1879.
2. Ibid.
3. Ibid.
4. Ibid.
5. *The Black Hills Weekly Times*, June 21, 1879.
6. Some historical records note his name was Len and not Lew.
7. https://www.ancestry.com/discoveryui-content/view/34566565:6742?tid=&pid
=&queryId=c2d0e36c57d91ede9c19efcb094877b4&_phsrc=kWk916&_phstart=success
Source; *The Black Hills Daily Times*, February 18, 1878; *The Black Hills Daily Times*,
November 22, 1879; *The Black Hills Daily Times*, March 5, 1880.
8. *The Black Hills Daily Times*, August 12, 1878; *The Daily Deadwood Pioneer Times*,
July 11, 1878.
9. *The Black Hills Daily Times*, August 27, 1879.
10. Ibid.
11. Ibid.
12. *The Black Hills Daily Times*, July 30, 1879; *The Black Hills Daily Times*, July 11,
1879.
13. Tollgate houses were erected at suitable intervals to collect tolls from wagon
drivers.
14. Ibid., July 12, 1879.
15. Ibid., September 26, 1879.
16. Ibid., November 4, 1879; South Dakota State Archives Miscellaneous Historical
Records Re: Deadwood.
17. *The Weekly Pioneer Times*, February 15, 1880; *The Black Hills Times*, July 11, 1879.
18. *The Weekly Pioneer Times*, February 15, 1880.
19. Ibid.
20. Ibid.
21. Ibid.
22. Ibid.
23. Ibid.
24. Ibid.
25. To become violent.
26. *The Weekly Pioneer Times*, February 15, 1880.
27. *The Black Hills Daily Times*, February 17, 1880; *The Black Hills Daily Times*, February 7, 1880.

28. *The Black Hills Daily Times*, February 13, 1880.
29. Ibid., June 13, 1882; *The Weekly Pioneer Times*, June 11, 1880.
30. *The Black Hills Daily Times*, May 29, 1880; *The Black Hills Daily Times*, May 30, 1880; *The Black Hills Weekly Times*, September 11, 1880.
31. *The Black Hills Weekly Times*, November 20, 1880.
32. *The Black Hills Daily Times*, January 21, 1881; *The Daily Deadwood Pioneer Times*, November 21, 1881.
33. *The Black Hills Daily Times*, February 10, 1881.
34. Ibid.
35. *The Weekly Pioneer Times*, May 5, 1881; *Press and Daily Dakotaian*, March 25, 1880; *The Daily Deadwood Pioneer*, September 16, 1881; *The Black Hills Daily Times*, September 22, 1881.
36. *The Black Hills Daily Times*, December 16, 1881.
37. Ibid.
38. Ibid.

CHAPTER 4

1. *Rapid City Journal*, December 21, 1928, and December 22, 1928.
2. Ibid.
3. Ibid., January 12, 1932, and January 9, 1932.
4. https://www.ancestry.com/discoveryui-content/view/59826965:7602?tid=&pid =&queryId=a8eb60602d07bfac6e1aeb5be205c792 &_phsrc=kWk917&_phstart=success Source; *Lead Daily Call*, August 5, 1909.
5. *The Daily Deadwood Pioneer Times*, February 5, 1904.
6. *Deadwood Magazine*, Winter 2004/2005.
7. *The Daily Deadwood Pioneer Times*, April 7, 1906.
8. Ibid.
9. Ibid.
10. *Argus Leader*, April 9, 1906.
11. *Rapid City Journal*, February 3, 1907.
12. Ibid., December 31, 1907; *Pierre Weekly Free Press*, March 26, 1908; *The Black Hills Union and Western Stock Review*, January 3, 1908; *Deadwood Magazine*, July/August 1994.
13. *Deadwood Magazine*, Winter 2004/2005; *Lead Daily Call*, August 5, 1909.
14. *Farmer's Almanac*, May/June 1909; Robert J. Casey, *The Black Hills and Their Incredible Characters: A Chronicle and a Guide* (Whitefish, MT: Literary Licensing, 2011), 44–46.
15. *The Black Hills*, 44–46.
16. *The Black Hills Weekly Journal*, July 25, 1913.
17. Ibid.
18. *Lead Daily Call*, November 8, 1913.
19. Ibid.
20. Ibid.
21. Ibid., December 24, 1913; *The Daily Deadwood Pioneer Times*, December 25, 1913.

22. *Deadwood Magazine,* Winter 2004/2005.
23. *Rapid City Journal,* October 11, 1918; *Deadwood Magazine,* Winter 2004/2005.
24. *Rapid City Journal,* February 8, 1920.
25. Ibid., December 13, 1983.
26. *Deadwood Magazine, Winter 2004/2005.*
27. Ibid.
28. Ibid.

CHAPTER 5

1. Chris Enss, *Wicked Women: Notorious, and Wayward Ladies from the Old West* (Guilford, CT: TwoDot Books, 2015), 40–45.
2. Ibid.
3. Ibid.
4. https://www.ancestry.com/discoveryui-content/view/503326619:7545?tid=&pid=&queryId=13667ab14eb242e9b7efda552934a7e7&phsrc=kWk918&phstart=success Source.
5. Ibid.
6. Enss, *Wicked Women,* 40–45.
7. Ibid.
8. Ibid.
9. Ibid.
10. Ibid.
11. https://www.ancestry.com/discoveryui-content/view/5033 26619:7545?tid=&pid=&queryId=13667ab14eb242e9b7efda552934a7e7&phsrc=kWk918&phstart=success Source; Enss, *Wicked Women,* 40–45.
12. Enss, *Wicked Women,* 40–45.
13. Ibid.
14. Ibid.
15. Ibid.
16. Ibid.
17. Ibid.
18. Ibid.
19. *Lead Daily Call,* July 28, 1967; *The Deadwood Pioneer Times,* July 28, 1961.
20. *The Mitchell Capital,* July 17, 1913.
21. Ibid.; *The Daily Deadwood Pioneer Times,* July 16, 1913.
22. *The Black Hills Weekly Times,* July 25, 1913.
23. *Argus Leader,* July 19, 1913; *Rapid City Journal,* July 18, 1913; *The Black Hills Journal,* July 25, 1913.
24. *Lead Daily Call,* February 21, 1924.
25. Ibid., June 10, 1924.
26. *Rapid City Journal,* June 6, 1927; *Rapid City Journal,* August 31, 1927; *The Daily Deadwood Pioneer Times,* September 29, 1927.
27. *Rapid City Journal,* June 6, 1927.
28. Ibid.

29. Ibid.
30. Ibid.
31. *The Daily Deadwood Pioneer Times*, December 3, 1927.
32. Ibid.
33. Ibid.
34. Ibid.
35. Ibid.
36. Ibid.
37. Ibid.
38. Ibid.
39. *Argus Leader*, October 9, 1928; *Lead Daily Call*, December 20, 1928.
40. *The Daily Deadwood Pioneer Times*, November 10, 1928.
41. *Rapid City Journal*, December 21, 1928.
42. Ibid., July 27, 1929.
43. *Argus Leaders*, October 8, 1929.
44. Ibid.
45. Ibid.
46. Ibid.
47. *The Daily Plainsman*, November 5, 1929, and November 21, 1929.
48. *The Black Hills Weekly Times*, February 8, 1930.

CHAPTER 6

1. *The Black Hills Daily Times*, March 21, 1894, and March 27, 1881; *The Black Hills Weekly Times*, April 2, 1881.
2. *The Daily Deadwood Pioneer Times*, December 19, 1893.
3. *The Weekly Pioneer Times*, March 8, 1894.
4. *The Black Hills Daily Times*, March 21, 1894.
5. *The Weekly Pioneer Times*, November 21, 1895.
6. *The Black Hills Daily Times*, April 19, 1892.
7. *Deadwood Evening Independent*, February 9, 1898.
8. Ibid.
9. Ibid.
10. *Lead Daily Call*, February 19, 1898.
11. *The Sisseton Weekly*, December 20, 1907.
12. Ibid.
13. Ibid.
14. *The Daily Deadwood Pioneer Times*, December 10, 1907.
15. Ibid.
16. Ibid.
17. Ibid.
18. Ibid.
19. Ibid.
20. Ibid.

21. https://www.ancestry.com/discoveryui-content/view/59827868:7602?tid=&pid=&queryId=958183d58e3dd3eff4445a2d1bdc2a28&_phsrc=kWk919&_phstart=success Source.

22. *The Daily Pioneer Times*, August 31, 1907.

CHAPTER 7

1. https://www.ancestry.com/discoveryui-content/view/229615:8561?tid=&pid=&queryId=a93320134d722be274a02e447c254fb2&_phsrc=kWk921&_phstart=success Source.

2. *The Weekly Yellowstone Journal and Livestock Reporter*, May 24, 1888.

3. *The Black Hills Daily Times*, August 18, 1885; *The Daily Deadwood Pioneer Times*, August 6, 1885.

4. *Rapid City Journal*, May 8, 1886.

5. Ibid., December 21, 1886.

6. *Argus Leader*, May 2, 1894; *Rapid City Journal*, September 21, 1886; Lewis Collins and Richard H. Collins, *Collins' Historical Sketches of Kentucky* (Greenville, SC: Southern Historical Press, 1979), 22.

7. *The Daily Deadwood Pioneer Times*, November 30, 1887.

8. South Dakota State Archives Miscellaneous Historical Records Re: Deadwood; *The Black Hills Daily Times*, August 22, 1888.

9. *Rapid City Journal*, October 14, 1888.

10. Ibid.

11. *The Black Hills Daily Times*, December 18, 1888; *Argus Leader*, December 24, 1888.

12. *Rapid City Journal*, July 26, 1881.

13. *The Black Hills Daily Times*, February 4, 1892.

14. Ibid.

15. Ibid., August 19, 1892; *Pierre Weekly Free Press*, July 20, 1893.

16. *Argus Leader*, May 2, 1894.

17. Ibid.

18. Ibid.

19. *The Black Hills Weekly Journal*, June 22, 1894; *Lead Daily Call*, May 17, 1895.

20. *The Black Hills Weekly Journal*, August 2, 1895.

21. *Rapid City Journal*, October 31, 1905.

22. *The Daily Deadwood Pioneer Times*, August 6, 1885; *The Daily Deadwood Pioneer Times*, December 5, 1885.

23. *The Black Hills Daily Times*, April 8, 1886.

24. Ibid., June 27, 1889.

25. *Pierre Weekly Free Press*, June 18, 1891, and April 5, 1894.

26. *Argus Leader*, September 25, 27, and 30, 1895; "Historic Places: Pierre & Fort Pierre," https://historicpierrefortpierre.com/; "Public Places," Shady Ladies of Missouri Avenue, https://historicpierrefortpierre.com/shady-ladies-of-missouri-avenue/.

CHAPTER 8

1. *Lead Daily Call, September* 3, 1908; *Argus Leader*, October 3, 1908.
2. Ibid.
3. Ibid.
4. *The Daily Deadwood Pioneer Times*, September 3, 1908.
5. Ibid.
6. *Lead Daily Call*, September 3, 1908; *The Daily Deadwood Pioneer Times*, September 4, 1908; *The Daily Deadwood Pioneer Times*, September 13, 1908; *The Black Hills Daily Register*, November 23, 1911.
7. *Argus Leader*, October 3, 1908.
8. *The Black Hills Daily Register*, October 15, 1910; *Lead Daily Call*, November 9, 1908.
9. *Argus Leader*, September 3, 1909.
10. Ibid.
11. *The Black Hills Daily Register*, November 23, 1911.
12. *The Daily Deadwood Pioneer Times*, November 24, 1911; *Lead Daily Call*, February 7, 1912.
13. *Lead Daily Call*, April 8, 1912, and October 29, 1912.
14. Ibid., October 30, 1912.
15. Ibid.
16. Ibid.
17. Ibid.
18. Ibid.
19. *The Daily Deadwood Pioneer Times*, October 31, 1912.

CHAPTER 9

1. *Black Hills Weekly Times*, March 3, 1894; *The Weekly Pioneer Times*, March 8, 1894.
2. Ibid.
3. Ibid.
4. Ibid.
5. Ibid.
6. Ibid.
7. Ibid.
8. Ibid.
9. Ibid., December 28, 1893; *The Mitchell Capital*, December 22, 1893.
10. *The Weekly Pioneer Times*, December 21, 1893.
11. Ibid.
12. *Black Hills Weekly Times*, March 3, 1894; *The Weekly Pioneer Times*, March 8, 1894.
13. Ibid.
14. Ibid.
15. *The Daily Pioneer Times*, January 12, 1894; *Rapid City Journal*, February 16, 1894.
16. Ibid.
17. Ibid.

18. Ibid.
19. Ibid.
20. Ibid.
21. Ibid.
22. Ibid.
23. Ibid.
24. Ibid.
25. Ibid.
26. Ibid.
27. Ibid.
28. Ibid.
29. Ibid.
30. *The Black Hills Weekly Journal*, March 16, 1894.
31. Ibid.
32. Ibid.
33. Ibid.
34. Ibid.
35. *Argus Leader*, April 10, 1899.

CHAPTER 10

1. *Funk & Wagnalls New Encyclopedia*, Vol. 9 1973.
2. https://www.ancestry.com/discoveryui-content/view/135789:8659?tid=&pid=&
queryId=ff0cd724d92219510a39b316c17abd89&_phsrc=kWk922&_phstart=success
Source.
3. South Dakota State Archives Miscellaneous Historical Records Re: Deadwood.
4. *The Daily Deadwood Pioneer Times*, June 7, 1921; *Lead Daily Call*, December 5,
1921; *The Weekly Pioneer Times*, September 12, 1929, and September 18, 1930.
5. *The Weekly Pioneer Times*, February 26, 1931.
6. Ibid.
7. https://www.ancestry.com/discoveryui-content/view/111986095:2442?tid=&pid
=&queryId=4825dff7b6f12f06153a2459240388a1&_phsrc=kWk923&_phstart=success
Source.
8. *Lead Daily Call*, July 31, 1928; *The Weekly Pioneer Times*, July 4, 1929.
9. Ibid., July 4, 1929, and February 24, 1934; *The Daily Deadwood Pioneer Times*, July
21, 1934.
10. *Lead Daily Call*, February 24, 1934; *Rapid City Times*, February 27, 1934.
11. *The Weekly Pioneer Times*, June 18, 1931, and December 6, 1934.
12. *Rapid City Journal*, May 21, 1936; *Lead Daily Call*, May 21, 1936.
13. https://www.ancestry.com/discoveryui-content/view/104681831:7884?tid=&pid
=&queryId=49a2f7613b592cf48a6a6d287b4b3521&_phsrc=kWk924&_phstart=success
Source.
14. South Dakota State Archives Miscellaneous Historical Records Re: Deadwood.
15. https://www.ancestry.com/discoveryui-content/view/69539608:6061?tid=&pid
=&queryId=0bc2eecc2e5dc5ad7a85af43c8d34185&_phsrc=kWk925&_phstart=success

Source; *The Daily Deadwood Pioneer Times*, February 2, 1943; *The Weekly Pioneer Times*, February 11, 1943.

16. *Star Tribune*, February 3, 1943; *The Minneapolis Star*, February 10, 1943; *St. Cloud Times*, April 3, 1943.

17. *The Daily Deadwood Pioneer Times*, October 7, 1949.

18. https://www.ancestry.com/discoveryui-content/view/8123849:62308?tid=&pid=&queryId=1be7ac49ee787b47bf45ac3faa3afd22&_phsrc=kWk926&_phstart=success Source.

19. *Lead Daily Call*, October 7, 1949.

20. *Rapid City Journal*, April 16, 1950, and September 13, 1951.

21. *Lead Daily Call*, July 29, 1951.

22. *Rapid City Journal*, July 29, 1951.

23. Ibid.

24. Ibid.

25. Ibid.

26. *The Daily Plainsman*, September 12, 1951.

27. *The Mitchell Daily Republic*, September 19, 1951.

28. Ibid.

29. Ibid.

30. Ibid.

31. Ibid.

32. *Argus Leader*, June 22, 1952.

33. Ibid.

34. Ibid.

35. Ibid., October 16, 1959.

36. Ibid.

37. Ibid.

38. A box in which customers placed their money for services rendered.

39. Ibid.

40. Ibid.

41. *Lead Daily Call*, September 28, 1960.

42. *Rapid City Journal*, January 30, 1960.

43. South Dakota State Archives Miscellaneous Historical Records Re: Deadwood.

44. Ibid.

45. Ibid.

46. *The Daily Deadwood Pioneer Times*, April 18, 1964; *Argus Leader*, May 10, 1964.

47. *The Daily Deadwood Pioneer Times*, April 10, 1973, December 18, 1970, January 29, 1972; *Lead Daily Call*, October 25, 1977.

48. *Argus Leader*, May 29, 1980.

49. Ibid., August 5, 1979, and August 6, 1979.

50. Ibid.

51. Ibid., August 10, 1979.

52. *The Black Hills Weekly Times*, June 11, 1980; *Argus Leader*, June 11, 1980.

53. *Lead Daily Call*, June 17, 1980.

54. Ibid.
55. Ibid.
56. Ibid.
57. Ibid
58. *Argus Leader*, September 12, 1980.
59. Ibid.
60. Ibid., October 4, 1980.
61. *Rapid City Journal*, October 8, 1980.
62. *Queen City Mail*, October 8, 1980.
63. *Rapid City Journal*, October 7, 1980, and October 8, 1980.
64. https://www.ancestry.com/discoveryui-content/view/8123849:62308?tid=&pid =&queryId=1be7ac49ee787b47bf45ac3faa3afd22&_phsrc=kWk926&_phstart=success Source.
65. *Lead Daily Call*, November 20, 1980.

CHAPTER 11

1. *Black Hills Monthly Magazine*, Vol. 1 No. 7 Spring 1980.
2. Ibid.
3. Ibid.
4. Ibid.; https://www.ancestry.com/discoveryui-content/view/141780964:60525 ?tid=&pid=&queryId=c3cb432d87ba88107986baeacd7081d6&_phsrc=kWk927&_ phstart=successSource.
5. https://www.ancestry.com/discoveryui-content/view/141780964:60525?tid=&pid =&queryId=c3cb432d87ba88107986baeacd7081d6&_phsrc=kWk927&_phstart=success Source.
6. *Argus Leader*, July 30, 1980; *The Black Hills Weekly Times*, July 16, 1980; *Black Hills Monthly Magazine*, Vol. 1 No. 7 Spring 1980.
7. Ibid.
8. *Argus Leader*, July 30, 1977.
9. Ibid.
10. *Argus Leader*, July 30, 1980.
11. *Black Hills Monthly Magazine*, Vol. 1 No. 7 Spring 1980.
12. Ibid.
13. Ibid.
14. Ibid.
15. Ibid.; *Lead Daily Call*, May 31, 1980.
16. *Lead Daily Call*, June 9, 1980.
17. Ibid.
18. *Lead Daily Call*, July 18, 1980; *Los Angeles Times*, July 20, 1980.
19. Ibid.
20. *Black Hills Monthly Magazine*, Vol. 1 No. 7 Spring 1980.
21. *Lead Daily Call*, July 18, 1980; *Standard Speaker*, July 19, 1980.
22. *Argus Leader*, November 21, 1980.

23. *The Black Hills Weekly Times*, March 4, 1981; *Black Hills Monthly Magazine*, Vol. 1 No. 7 Spring 1980.

24. *Rapid City Journal*, April 12, 1982; *Lead Daily Call*, May 29, 1984.

25. *The Tampa Tribune*, February 17, 1982; https://www.ancestry.com/discoveryui -content/view/141780964:60525?tid=&pid=&queryId=c3cb432d87ba88107986baeacd7 081d6&_phsrc=kWk927&_phstart=successSource.

26. Ibid.

CHAPTER 12

1. https://www.ancestry.com/discoveryui-content/view/265766:60162?tid=&pid=&q ueryId=81d6504a9a6c8054aee6ddbe72fbc640&_phsrc=nJE92&_phstart=successSource.

2. https://www.ancestry.com/discoveryui-content/view/512390:60162?tid=&pid=& queryId=118a5cd7ef05b53d0c90ad5fae7fc3e5&_phsrc=nJE94&_phstart=successSource.

3. *The Weekly Pioneer-Times*, December 8, 1932.

4. *Deadwood Pioneer-Times*, November 5, 1934.

5. Ibid., February 4, 1936.

6. https://www.ancestry.com/discoveryui-content/view/122164088:6224?tid=&pid =&queryId=dda7fce26b0ed3cc709af64ef79f5bec&_phsrc=nJE95&_phstart=success Source.

7. *Lead Daily Call*, May 6, 1935.

8. *The Daily Deadwood Pioneer-Times*, August 9, 1891.

9. Ibid., September 8, 1929.

10. *The Weekly Pioneer-Times*, September 18, 1941.

11. Ibid., April 2, 1943.

12. *Lead Daily Call*, July 3, 1961.

13. *The Black Hills Weekly Times*, October 14, 1949; *Deadwood Pioneer-Times*, October 7, 1949.

14. *Deadwood Pioneer-Times*, July 29, 1951, *Argus Leader*, July 29, 1951

15. *Rapid City Journal*, June 22, 1952; *Deadwood Pioneer-Times*, June 22, 1951.

16. *Daily Republic*, October 16, 1959; *Argus Leader*, October 22, 1959.

17. *Deadwood Pioneer-Times*, October 16, 1959.

18. *The Daily Plainsman*, March 20, 1960.

19. *Lead Daily Call*, September 28, 1960.

20. *Argus Leader*, April 19, 1964.

21. *Lead Daily Call*, May 8, 1964.

22. https://www.ancestry.com/discoveryui-content/view/52003:60161?tid=&pid=& queryId=65d15bd4952793c730d19bf3dda7fad8&_phsrc=nJE96&_phstart=success Source.

23. *Deadwood Pioneer-Times*, June 24, 1957.

24. *The Weekly Pioneer-Times*, February 22, 1934.

25. *Rapid City Journal*, May 22, 1936; *Lead Daily Call*, May 21, 1936.

26. *The Black Hills Weekly*, October 14, 1949; *Lead Daily Call*, October 7, 1949.

27. *Lead Daily Call*, July 29, 1951; *Deadwood Pioneer-Times*, July 29, 1951.

28. *Deadwood Pioneer-Times*, July 29, 1951.

29. Ibid., June 22, 1952; *Rapid City Journal,* June 21, 1952, and July 21, 1952.
30. *The Black Hills Weekly Times,* October 21, 1959; *Argus-Leader,* October 16, 1959.
31. *Argus-Leader,* October 16, 1959.
32. *Argus-Leader,* December 23, 1959.
33. *The Black Hills Weekly Times,* March 31, 1965.
34. *Lead Daily Call,* April 13, 1967.
35. *Deadwood Pioneer-Times,* January 27, 1932.
36. Ibid., April 16, 1932.
37. *The Weekly Pioneer-Times,* August 18, 1932.
38. https://www.ancestry.com/discoveryui-content/view/17409657:60901?tid=&pid
=&queryId=8c0449783d1c297b6f204e2ea857a268&_phsrc=nJE97&_phstart=success
Source; *Star Tribune,* August 12, 2003.
39. Ibid.; *The Black Hills Weekly,* July 16, 1980.
40. *Deadwood Pioneer-Times,* February 2, 1943.
41. *Rapid City Journal,* December 11, 1995.
42. *Deadwood Pioneer-Times,* January 18, 1941.
43. *Rapid City Journal,* September 19, 1982.
44. *Lead Daily Call,* May 21, 1936.
45. *Rapid City Journal,* January 18, 1951.
46. https://www.ancestry.com/discoveryui-content/view/16921
1827:62308?tid=&pid=&queryId=6ffffdfb6430504e81d36e3a155
f8c56&_phsrc=nJE98&_phstart=successSource.
47. *Rapid City Journal,* May 10, 1935.
48. *Deadwood Pioneer-Times,* July 3, 1935; *Rapid City Journal,* July 5, 1935.
49. https://www.ancestry.com/discoveryui-content/view/52003:60161?tid=&pid=&
queryId=65d15bd4952793c730d19bf3dda7fad8&_phsrc=nJE96&_phstart=success
Source.
50. *Lead Daily Call,* October 7, 1949.
51. Ibid., July 29, 1951.
52. Ibid.
53. *Argus Leader,* June 22, 1952.
54. *Deadwood Pioneer-Times,* October 16, 1959.
55. Ibid.
56. *Lead Daily Call,* September 28, 1960.
57. Ibid., April 18, 1964; *Rapid City Journal,* May 8, 1964.
58. *Lead Daily Call,* May 21, 1936; *Deadwood Pioneer-Times,* May 22, 1936.
59. *Deadwood Pioneer-Times,* January 3, 1938.
60. Ibid., March 27, 1937.
61. *Lead Daily Call,* January 17, 1939.
62. *Rapid City Journal,* July 29, 1951; *Argus-Leader,* August 2, 1951.
63. *Rapid City Journal,* August 8, 1951.
64. Ibid., June 21, 1952.
65. Ibid., October 16, 1959.
66. *Deadwood Pioneer-Times,* September 28, 1960.

67. *Lead Daily Call*, April 18, 1964; *Rapid City Journal*, May 8, 1964.

68. https://www.ancestry.com/discoveryui-content/view/228281:8561?tid=&pid=& queryId=1527576255a3c3783c6df9c4517d3a56&_phsrc=nJE99&_phstart=success Source.

69. *Lead Daily Call*, March 31, 1936.

70. Ibid., August 5, 1936.

71. *Deadwood Pioneer-Times*, May 22, 1936.

72. *Rapid City Journal*, August 28, 1937.

73. *Lead Daily Call*, October 12, 1937.

74. *Rapid City Journal*, November 30, 1942.

75. Ibid., October 25, 1992.

76. *Deadwood Pioneer-Times*, May 22, 1936.

77. *Lead Daily Call*, October 5, 1937.

78. *Deadwood Pioneer-Times*, October 29, 1932.

79. Ibid., June 4, 1933.

80. Ibid., May 8, 1934.

81. Ibid., July 16, 1934; *The Weekly Pioneer-Times*, July 26, 1934.

82. *Deadwood Pioneer-Times*, October 17, 1934.

83. *Rapid City Journal*, June 16, 1989; https://www.ancestry.com/discoveryui-content/ view/79243354:60525?tid=&pid=&queryId=cdb135a7f634ebe2cf927831e2d9d810&_ phsrc=nJE100&_phstart=successSource.

84. *Argus Leader*, May 22, 1980, and October 7, 1980.

85. *Lead Daily Call*, October 9, 1980.

86. https://www.ancestry.com/discoveryui-content/view/17409657:60901?tid=&pid =&queryId=8c0449783d1c297b6f204e2ea857a268&_phsrc=nJE97&_phstart=success Source; *Star Tribune*, August 12, 2003.

87. Ibid.

88. *Argus Leader,* May 22, 1980, and October 7, 1980.

89. *Lead Daily Call*, October 9, 1980.

90. *Argus Leader*, May 22, 1980, and October 7, 1980.

91. *Lead Daily Call*, October 9, 1980.

BIBLIOGRAPHY

BOOKS

Aikman, Duncan. *Calamity Jane and the Lady Wildcats.* Lincoln: University of Nebraska Press, 1927.

————. *Madam Mustache and Other Gaming Ladies.* New York: Henry Holt & Company, 1927.

Brown, Dee. *The Gentle Tamers: Women of the Old Wild West.* Lincoln: University of Nebraska Press, 1958.

Byrant, Jerry L. and Barbara Fifer. *Deadwood's Al Swearingen: Manifest Evil in the Gem Theatre.* Helena, MT: FarCountry Press, 2018.

————. *Deadwood Saints and Sinners.* Helena, MT: FarCountry Press, 2016.

Casey, Robert J. *The Black Hills and Their Incredible Characters: A Chronicle and a Guide.* Whitefish, MT: Literary Licensing, 2011.

Collins, Lewis and Richard H. Collins. *Collins' Historical Sketches of Kentucky.* Greenville, SC: Southern Historical Press, 1979.

Drago, Harry S. *Notorious Ladies of the Frontier.* New York: Ballantine Books, 1972.

Enss, Chris. *Wicked Women: Notorious, and Wayward Ladies from the Old West.* Guilford, CT: TwoDot Books, 2015.

Fielder, Mildred. *Poker Alice.* Deadwood, SD: Centennial Distributors, 1978.

Hegne, Barbara. *Harlots, Hurdies & Spirited Women of Virginia City, Nevada.* Medford, OR: FreeStyle Graphics, 2001.

Janicot, Michael. *The Ladies of the Night: A Short History of Prostitution in Nevada County, California.* Nevada City, CA: Mountain House Press, 1986.

McClintock, John S. and Edward L. Seen. *Pioneer Days in the Black Hills: Accurate History and Facts Related By One of the Early Day Pioneers.* Norman: University of Oklahoma Press, 2000.

Mezulla, Fred and Jo Mezulla. *Outlaw Albums.* Denver, CO: A. D. Hirschfield Press, 1966.

Rezatto, Helen. *Tales of the Black Hills.* Rapid City, SD: Fenwyn Press, 1989.

Ross, Edward A. *Madam Mustache: Pioneer of the Parlor House Circuit.* Cleveland, OH: Quirk Books, 1981.

Trump, Michael. *Raiding Deadwood's Bad Lands: It's Illegal History of Prostitution and Gambling.* Deadwood, SD: The Adams Museum & House, Inc., 2009.

NEWSPAPERS

The Aberdeen Democrat, Aberdeen, South Dakota, April 13, 1906

Argus Leader, Sioux Falls, South Dakota

The Arizona Daily Sun, Flagstaff, Arizona
Bismarck Weekly, Bismarck, North Dakota
Black Hills Champion, Deadwood, South Dakota
The Black Hills Daily Register, Lead, South Dakota
The Black Hills Daily Times, Deadwood, South Dakota
The Black Hills Union and Western Stock Review, Rapid City, South Dakota
Black Hills Weekly Herald, Deadwood, South Dakota
The Black Hills Weekly Journal, Deadwood, South Dakota
The Black Hills Weekly Journal, Rapid City, South Dakota
The Black Hills Weekly Pioneer, Deadwood, South Dakota
The Black Hills Weekly Times, Deadwood, South Dakota
The Black Hills Union, Rapid City, South Dakota
The Bodie Daily Free Press, Bodie, California
Daily Champion, Deadwood, South Dakota
The Daily Deadwood Pioneer Times, Deadwood, South Dakota
The Daily Plainsman, Huron, South Dakota
Daily Republic, Mitchell, South Dakota
The Deadwood Evening Independent, Deadwood, South Dakota
Deadwood Pioneer Times, Deadwood, South Dakota
Frank Leslie's Weekly Newspaper, New York, New York
The Herald, Oskaloosa, Iowa
Lead Daily Call, Lead, South Dakota
Los Angeles Times, Los Angeles, California
The Minneapolis Journal, Minneapolis, Minnesota
The Minneapolis Star, Minneapolis, Minnesota
The Mitchell Capital, Mitchell, South Dakota
The Mitchell Daily Republic, Mitchell, South Dakota
The Mountain Messenger, Downieville, California
The Nebraska State Journal, Lincoln, Nebraska
Oakland Tribune, Oakland, California
Pierre Weekly Free Press, Pierre, South Dakota
Press and Daily Dakotaian, Yankton, Dakota Territory
Queen City Mail, Spearfish, South Dakota
Rapid City Journal, Rapid City, South Dakota
St. Cloud Times, St. Cloud, Minnesota
The St. Louis Star and Times, St. Louis, Missouri
The Sisseton Weekly, Roberts County, South Dakota
The Standard Speaker, Hazelton, Pennsylvania
Star Tribune, Minneapolis, Minnesota
The Tampa Tribune, Tampa, Florida
The Telegraph Forum, Bucyrus, Ohio
The Weekly Pioneer Times, Deadwood, South Dakota
The Weekly Yellowstone Journal and Livestock Reporter, Miles City, Montana

HISTORICAL ARCHIVES/MAGAZINES/ENCYCLOPEDIA

Adams Banner Newsletter, Adams Museum, Deadwood, South Dakota
Black Hills Monthly Magazine
Deadwood Magazine
Farmer's Almanac
Funk & Wagnalls New Encyclopedia
South Dakota State Archives, Miscellaneous Historical Records Re: Deadwood

WEBSITES

ancestry.com
encyclopedia.com/women/
historicpierrefortpierre.com/
legendsofamerica.com/

INDEX

abortion, 101
abuse: at Gem Variety Theater,
23–27, 32–33; of Swearingen,
N., 26
Ace High Rooms, 146
actresses, prostitutes claiming to
be, 11
Adams Museum, 157
alcohol, 95; high-grade, 123; illegal
sale of, 123; legally selling,
122; liquor license, 129;
moonshine, 77; possessing
and selling, 121; theft of, 96
Allen, Judy, 153
Alton, Kitty, 25–26
Anderson, Sandy, 153
Annex Rooms, 124, *125*, 147–48
Arcade Rooms, 146–47, 151–52
Argus Leader, 128–29, 132, 134; on
Brown, M., 98–99; on World
Series, 81
Arndt, Winifred, 154
arrests, 12, 58, 98, 124, 127,
129; of Big Jess, 65; of
Campbell, T., 103, 106; of
Copas, 122; of Desmond,
33; as discriminatory, 16; of
DuFran, D., 63; of Fletcher,
131, 133; of Holliday, 139;
of Ivers, 76–77, 80; of

Lashley, 66; of Lee, 100;
of Longland, P., 121; of
McMahon, 6; of Popcorn
Jenny, 7; for solicitation, 65;
of Spencer, 51; of Stacy, 56;
of Swearingen, E., 24–25, 39;
of Tilford, 96; of Trevyr, 111;
of Ward, W., 56
Askine, Frank, 105
assaults, 11–13, 66; of Bell, G.,
122–23

Bad Lands, 5, *6*, 16, 83; main
thoroughfare from, *14*
Baird, Alice S., 101
Baldwin, Billy, 154
Ballenger, Tony, 153
baseball, 80–81
Beer Barrel Barn, *141*
Beige Door, 155–56, 157
Belding, John P., 11, 12
Bell, Flora, 50, 51
Bell, Gertrude (Leaty),
122–23, 148
Bella Union, 43, 51
Belle Fourche, 62–63, 87, 88
Bennett, Anna, 57
Bernard, Prentice. *See* Vinegar
Rowan
Big Jess, 65

Black, Sally, 147
Black Hills, 3, 10
Black Hills Daily Times, 32, 39;
    on Brown, M., 97; on Gem
    Variety Theater, 29–30,
    34–36; on Haskell, 86; on
    Johnson, 52, 53, 57, 58; on
    social evil, 9; on Swearingen,
    E., 33, 37
Black Hills Monthly Magazine,
    140, 143
Black Hills Union, 11
Black Hills Weekly Herald, 13
Black Hills Weekly Journal, 65
Black Hills Weekly Pioneer Times:
    on DeBelloy, 112; on Gem
    Variety Theater, 22, 29; on
    Johnson, 54–55; on Perry, 38;
    on Trevyr, 115–17
Black Hills Weekly Times, 14; on
    Johnson, 57; on LeRoy and
    Curley murder-suicide, 28;
    on Sexton, 32
blackjack, 44, 47
Bodega Rooms, 119
Bolger, Ned, 123
Bolshaw, Amy Helen Dorothea.
    See DuFran, Dora
Brandenburg, R. E., 134, 150
Bright, Lottie, 95
Broadwater, Maggie, 90–92
The Brothel Deadwood, 157–58
brothels. *See specific topics*
Brown, Charlie, 150

Brown, May, 93–95; death of, 100;
    divorce of, 97; fire and, 99;
    Tilford and, 96–97, 98–99
Brownell, Dee, 153
Bruce, Lena, 32
Bruno, Mickey (Pearl Marie
    Melton), 124, 148, 149, 151
Bryant, Frank, 1
Bullock, Seth, 9
Bulow, William J., 80
Burke, Jackie, 153–54
Burns, Johnny, 23

Calamity Jane (Martha Jane
    Canary), 5, 25–26, 62, *67*
Campbell, Betty J. *See* Holliday,
    Pam
Campbell, Thelma: arrests of, 103,
    106; court cases and, 103–7;
    fire and, 104–5, *105*; suicide
    attempted by, 106
Canary, Martha Jane. *See* Calamity
    Jane
Carnahan, William, 130
Carpenter, Thelma, 123
carriage accident, 50–51
Carroll, Jacki, 151
Carver, Dutch, 44
Casey, Robert, 64
"cat house," 139
Chicago Cubs, 80
Chicago World's Fair (1933), 68
China Doll (DiGee), 6, 7

churches, 9; Fellowship Baptist
Church, 134; St. Ambrose
Catholic Church, 122
City Council of Deadwood, 9
Clark, Cleo, 66
Clark, Ida, 33
Clark, Thomas, 25
Collins, Jean, 147
Coney Island (brothel), 64, 66
Conway, Kitty, 34
Cooley and Doherty Opera
House, 56
Cooper, Courtney Ryley, 77
Cooper, Pat, 128–29, 130, 152, 153
Cooperman, M. J. "Curley," 154
Copas, Wayne "Whitey,"
122–23, 148
Copperman, Alice, 146
court cases, 131–32; Campbell, T.,
and, 103–7; DuFran, D., and,
61–62; Fletcher and, 133;
Holliday and, 143; Ivers and,
76–77; Johnson and, 56; Lee
and, 100; Trevyr and, 113–18
Cowbelles, 138
Cox, Tommie/Tommy, 135, 139,
139, 155
Cozy Rooms, 119, 122–24, 131,
139, 148–49
Cricket Saloon, 21–22
Crotty, Charles, 134
Curley, Sam, 27, 28
Curruthers, Florence R., 16
Custer City, 21, 26

Daily Champion, 5, 7
Daily Deadwood Pioneer Times,
15–17, 26, 63; on Campbell,
T., 104; on McDermott, 85
Dakota Territory, 9, 49
Daly, Marty Jones, 149
Daly Rooms, 149
Davis, Maggie, 12
Days of '76 Museum, 157
Deadwood, *42, 50*; busy, *2*; early
days of, *110*; main street of, *3,
121*. *See also specific topics*
Deadwood City Council, 12
Deadwood Evening Independent, 87
Deadwood Historic Preservation
Commission, 157
Deadwood History, Inc.
(DHI), 157
Deadwood Pioneer Times, 4,
125, 131
Deadwood Woman's Vigilance
Committee, 13
Deane, Dora, 115
deaths, 13; of Broadwater, 92; of
Brown, M., 100; of DuFran,
D., 68; of DuFran, J., 64; of
Fletcher, 135; of Holliday,
143; of Ivers, 82; of Lee,
100–101; of Longland,
P., 122; of Phillips, 53; of
Swearingen, E., 40. *See also*
murders; suicides
DeBelloy, Frank, 85, 109–13, 115
Denver Post, 77
Desmond, Lou, 33

DHI. *See* Deadwood History, Inc.
Diddlin' Dora's, 62
DiGee. *See* China Doll
directory, 146–56
divorce, of Brown, M., 97
Doe, Blanche, 97
Donahue, Phil, 142
Donovan, Michael, 114
Dority, Dan, 23
Douglas, Fannie, 33
drugs, rules against, 140
Duffield, Frank, 72
DuFran, Dora, *60*, 61–68
DuFran, Joseph, 62
Dumont, Eleanora "Madame
    Mustache," 41–47, *43*
DuPont, Parks, 152
Dutch Ann, 36

"Easy Come, Easy Go" (Ivers),
    77–80
Evans, Barbara, 149
Evans, Judy, 152

Fairmont Hotel, *91*
Fallon, Dell, 45
Federal Bureau of Investigation
    (FBI), 124, 137, 142
Fellowship Baptist Church, 134
Fern's Place, 119
Fillbach, Rose, 77
fines, 11, 12, 15, 63, 64
fires: Brown, M., and, 99;
    Campbell, T., and, 104–5,
    105; DuFran, D., and, 63; at

Gem Variety Theater, 29, 40;
    Johnson and, 56–57
Fitzgerald, John E., Jr., 141
Fletcher, Hazel Ione "Dixie,"
    123–26, *126*, 128, 130, 139,
    148, 151–52, 156; arrest of,
    131, 133; case against, 133;
    death of, 135; liquor license
    of, 129
Fort Meade, 49, 75, 77
the 400 (bordello), 83, 85, 86,
    87, 115
Fowler, Benny, 88–89
Frank Leslie's Weekly, 8
Frawley, Henry, 113
Frontier Rooms, 131, 150
Furze, Richard, 128

gamblers, 8; Ivers as, 72–73
gambling dens, 3, 9, 43, 72
Gardner, Harry, 155
Gem Variety Theater, 11, 19–40,
    21, 109, 111, 119; abuse and
    violence at, 23–27, 32–33;
    audience members at, 34–35;
    Conway at, 34; customers
    at bar of, *26*; decor of, 31;
    fire at, 29, 40; interior of, *22*;
    murder-suicides at, 28–29,
    35; popularity of, 22–23;
    publicity of, 34; reopening of,
    29–30; second floor of, 19;
    Sexton at, 31–32; unknown
    prostitute at, *20*
Gertie, 36

Gilbert, F. G., 66
Ginter, Iva, 146
Gold Dust Gambling House, 72
gold rush, 1, 43, 72
Gordon, Kay (Mary Putnam),
    128–29, 148, 149
Gotsch, Johanne, 93
Gotsch, Ottoman, 93
Gran, Beverly, 128–29
Gray, Beverly, 147
Green Door, *124*, 156
Green Front Theater, *4*, 119

Hamilton, Frank, 95
Hamilton, John, 96
Hamilton, May, 98
Hanley, Harold R., 61
Hardesty, Jack "Lucky," 72–73
Hard Scrabbles, 49
Harnett, Hattie, 56
Harris, James, 87
Haskell, Belle, 83–92, 109, 111,
    112, 115, 118; McDermott
    and, 83, 85; Stanley and, 85;
    wealth of, 86
Hastings (Attorney General), 113
Havens, Rebecca, 150
Headquarters Saloon, 96
Heddon, Richard P., 149
Henderson, Minnie, 103–5
Herring, Betty, 147
Hickok, James Butler, 5
Hickok, Wild Bill, 74
high-grade alcohol, 123
Hines, Jenny (Popcorn Jenny), 6–7

Historic Adams House, 157
Hizer, Annie (Little
    Buttercup), 56
Hodges, Joe, 7
Hoffman, Coney, 58
Hogan, Flora, 95
Holliday, Pam (Betty J. Campbell),
    137, 150, 156; arrest of,
    139; background of, 138;
    business holdings of, 139;
    "cat house" of, 139; death of,
    143; evidence photo, *131*;
    opinions on prostitution, 135;
    photograph of, 138
Homestake Adams Research and
    Cultural Center, 157
Howard, May, 95
Huckert, George, 74
Huntley, Marvin, 155
hurdy-gurdy houses, 5

Irwin, Elsie L. *See* Cox, Tommie
Ivers, Alice (Poker Alice), 69–82,
    70, *71*; arrests of, 76–77, 80;
    background of, 70–71; death
    of, 82; "Easy Come, Easy Go"
    by, 77–80; façade of brothel
    owned by, *75*; marksmanship
    of, 74; murder by, 76; as
    professional gambler, 72–73;
    reputation of, 73; at World
    Series, 80–81

James, Otie, 13
Janklow, William, 132

Jay, Lodell, 152
Jefferson, Thomas, 31
Jenks, Ann, 147
Jerome, Jerry, 151
Johnson, Mollie, 49–59;
    background of, 51; business
    of, 53; community support by,
    54; fire and, 56–57
Jones, Thomas, 65

Kansas City Star, 77
K Company, 76
Keil, Catherine, 147
Kelley, Mike, 152
Kelley, Pat, 149
Keough, Inez, 146
King, Georgia, 96
Klide, Kitty, 35–36
Koetzle, Fred, 75–76

Lackous, O. C., 113, 114
LaDeaux, Catherine, 155
ladies at bordello, *52*
Lamm, Lavinia, 155
Larson, Shirley, 149
Lashley, Charles, 66
"The Last Rose of Summer," 31
law enforcement, 15, 87, 126, 128,
    137; dishonesty of, 8; Hines
    raided by, 6–7; Ivers and, 77;
    raids by, 6–7, 16; Swearingen,
    E., and, 25; Tilford and, 96,
    98; train robbery and, 96
lawlessness, of Deadwood, 3–4
Lawrence, Robert, 96

Lead Daily Call, 106, 132, 133
Lee, Maud, 100–101
LeRoy, Kitty, 27–28
licensing system, 14–15
lightning strike, fire from, 99
liquor license, of Fletcher, 129
Little Buttercup. *See* Hizer, Annie
Lone Star Saloon, 28
Longland, Burr, 121
Longland, Pauline, 121–22
Love, Irene, *120*
Low Down on Calamity Jane
    (DuFran, D.), 68

madams: Brown, M., 93–100;
    DuFran, D., *60*, 61–68;
    Dumont, 41–47, *43*; Johnson,
    49–59; licenses for, 14;
    security guards for, 15. *See
    also* Haskell, Belle; Holliday,
    Pam; Ivers, Alice
Main Street Initiative
    Committee, 157
Mann Act, 106, 123
Mansion Hotel and Bar, 88
marksmanship, of Ivers, 74
Mascott Saloon, 83, 85, 109, 114
McCall, Jack, 74
McClintock, John S., 24
McDermott, Maggie, 83, 85,
    109–18
McDonald, Mary A. "Baby," 19
McGrath, Richard, 126
McKnight, Jack, 46
McMahon, Belle, 6

McMillen, Barbara Lee, 148, 149
Mecca Rooms, 150
Meer, Jonathan, 113
Melton, Pearl Marie. *See* Bruno, Mickey
Melville, May, 95–96
Meyer, Dr. C. W., 56
Meyer, Richard H., 130
Miller, Michelle, 147
Minard, E. E., 151
The Mine, 28
Miner, Joseph C., 76
Mitchell, Frank, 146
Mitchell, Maggie "Big Mag," 33
Mitchell Daily Republic, 127–28
Mook, Languare, 146
moonshine, 77
Moore, Ellen Lucille "Big Lu," 123–24, 150
Moran, Dick, 88–90
Moulds, James, 130
Mount Moriah Cemetery, 53, 64, 68, 92
murders: by Ivers, 76; of McDermott, 83, 85, 109–18; of Moran, 89–90; murder-suicides, 28–29, 35
Murfin (Captain), 113
Murphy, Geraldine, 151
Murphy, John, 149
Myers, Betty, 153

National Prohibition Act (Volstead Act), 119, 122

necessary evil, prostitution as, 5, 123
Nevada Journal, 45
Never Sweats, 49
Nifty Rooms, 150
Nugget, LLC, 157

Oates Opera Company, 31
O'Hara, Myrtle "Mert," 152–53
Old Abe Mine, 25
O'Leary, P. H., 98
Olsen, Arthur, 65–66
Olson, Alice, 61

Paine, Lizzie, 13
Pam's Other Door, 142
pandemic, Spanish influenza (1918), 66
Pearl Saloon, 23
Peasley, Lizzie, 33
Pennington County Health Unit, 126
Perry, Loudella, 38
Pettijohn, Miss, 58
Philadelphia Athletics, 80
Phillips, Jennie (Josephine Willard), 53
Phoenix Rooms, 151
Piergue, Anna. *See* Brown, May
Piergue, Edward, 93
Pine Rooms, 124, 131, 151–52
Pioneer Auto Museum, 142
Pioneer Days in the Black Hills (McClintock), 24
Piper, Vivian, 155

Plowman, Jeffrey W., 114, 117
Poker Alice. *See* Ivers, Alice
police. *See* law enforcement
Polk, Lou, 10
Popcorn Jenny. *See* Hines, Jenny
Potter, Bulah, 39
Press and Daily Dakotaian, 29
prison, Ivers in, 80
prostitution. *See specific topics*
Purcell, Clyde, 147
Purple Door, 135, 137, 138, 140, *141*, 142, 156
Putnam, Mary. *See* Gordon, Kay

"Queen of the Blondes." *See* Johnson, Mollie

Rapid City Journal, 64, 95, 126–27; on DuFran, D., 66–68; on Ivers, 77, 80; on Swearingen, E., 40; on Tilford, 97
Reed, Alban, 122
Reid, Cora, 152
respectable women, 13
Rice, Hattie, 109, 111, 114
Rosie's Place, 119
Russell, Ruby, 147
Rypkema, Eddie, 124–25, 147

Sabbath, 9
Salvation Army, 87
Saturday Evening Post, 77
Scott, Ann, 152
Scott, Gale, 153
security force, 15

Sessions, Mrs. I., 13
Sexton, Inez, 31–32
Shasta Rooms, 131, 152–53, 157
Shultz, Delphine, 146
Shy-Ann Rooms, 153–54
slavery, white, 106, 123–24
Smith, Boots, 152
Smith, Mattie, 95
Smith, Mollie, 98
Snell, Laverta "Babe," 152
Snyder, Shirley, 149
social evil, prostitution as, 9
soiled doves, 6, 10, 11, *17*, 50, 83
solicitation, arrests for, 65
South Deadwood Hose Company, 56
Spanish influenza pandemic (1918), 66
Sparrow, Kitty "Tricks," 23
Spencer, Lew, 51
sporting girls, 3
sporting women, 12
Stacy, Charlie, 56
stagecoaches, *86*
St. Ambrose Catholic Church, 122
Stanley, Nellie, 85
Star Bakery, 29
suicides, 24, 41, 85; attempted by Broadwater, 90; attempted by Campbell, T., 106; murder-suicides, 28–29, 35; of Perry, 38
Summers, Mickie, 151
Swearingen, Ellis Albert "Al," 19–40, *30*, 62, 63, 111;

abuse of prostitutes by, 23–24; arrests of, 24–25, 39; background of, 21; death of, 40; law enforcement and, 25; *Rapid City Journal* on, 40
Swearingen, Nettie, 21–22, 26

tax evasion, 143
taxpayers, 14
Taylor, Jean, 147
Taylor, Jessie, 65
telephone surveys, 132
theft, 57; of alcohol, 96; train robbery, 96–97
Thomas, Phatty, 1
The Three Nickels, 154
Tilford, John, 96–97, 98–99
Tobin, David, 46
Today Show, 142
Torrence, W. W., 85
train robbery, 96–97
Trevyr, Austie (Mary Yusta), 83, 85, 109–18
trials. *See* court cases
Trimpy, Edward, 23–24
Tubbs, Alice. *See* Ivers, Alice
Tubbs, Warren G., 69, 73–74
Turner, Vickie, 151

United States Department of Justice, 106
United States Marshals Service, 137
unknown prostitute, *20, 108*
Utter, Charlie, 5

venereal diseases, 126
Vinegar Rowan (Prentice Bernard), 88–89
Virginia Rooms, 154
Volstead Act. *See* National Prohibition Act

Waite (editor of *Nevada Journal*), 45, 46
Waldon, Lora, 11
Ward, Ginger, 147
Ward, William, 56
WCTU. *See* Woman's Christian Temperance Union
Weber, Carolyn, 157–58
Welch, Pat, 153–54
Westover, Beatrice, 153
Wheeler, Bea, 124, 130, 147–48
White Door, 156
white slavery, 106, 123–24
Willard, Josephine. *See* Phillips, Jennie
Williams, Dick, 100
Willis, Oscar, 31
Wilson, Charley, 35
Wilson, Karen, 149
Winner Rooms, 155
Winters, Florence, 11
Wirtz, Pauline. *See* Longland, Pauline
Witherspoon, James E., 58
Woman's Christian Temperance Union (WCTU), 15–16
Woodall, Miss, 58
Woods, Anna (Annie), 103, 106

World Series, 80–81

World's Fair, Chicago (1933), 68

Wright, Bessie, 65

Yellow Pages, 131

Yusta, Mary. *See* Trevyr, Austie

ABOUT THE AUTHOR

Chris Enss is a *New York Times* best-selling author who has been writing about women of the Old West for more than twenty years. She has penned more than forty published books on the subject. Her work has been honored with six Will Rogers Medallion Awards, two Elmer Kelton Book Awards, the Downing Journalism Award, and an Oklahoma Center for the Book Award. Enss's most recent works are *According to Kate: The Legendary Life of Big Nose Kate, Love of Doc Holliday, Iron Women: The Ladies Who Helped Build the Railroad*, and *The Widowed Ones: Beyond the Battle of the Little Bighorn*. She lives in Grass Valley, California.